The Great
Chicago
Trivia
& Fact
Book

The Great **Chicago** Trivia & Fact Book

Connie Goddard
and
Bruce Hatton Boyer

CUMBERLAND HOUSE
NASHVILLE, TENNESSEE

In memory of my father, Don Heaton,
who came to Chicago to see the Century of Progress
and never left—and would also share his enthusiasm for
the city with anyone who would listen.
—CHG—

For Janice, Sam, and Lydia.
—BHB—

Copyright © 1996 by Connie Goddard and Bruce Hatton Boyer
All rights reserved.

Published by Cumberland House Publishing, Inc., 2200 Abbott Martin Road, Suite 102, Nashville, Tennessee 37215.

Distributed to the trade by Andrews and McMeel, 4900 Main Street, Kansas City, Missouri 64112.

Cover by Will Owens.
Design by Harriette Bateman.

Library of Congress Cataloging-in-Publication Data
Goddard, Connie, 1943-
    The Great Chicago trivia and fact book / Connie Goddard and Bruce Hatton Boyer.
        p.   cm.
    Includes bibliographical references (p.   ).
    ISBN 1-888952-07-5 (pbk. : alk. paper)
    1. Chicago (Ill..)--Miscellanea.   I. Title.
    F548.3G63   1996
    977.3'11'00202--dc20   96-35900
                                                                                    CIP

Printed in the United States of America
1 2 3 4 5 6 7 — 00 99 98 97 96

CONTENTS

ACKNOWLEDGMENTS

We are, naturally, in debt to several people who have written both informal and scholarly histories of Chicago. We borrowed rather liberally from some, particularly those of Kenan Heise, Richard Lindberg, and June Skinner Sawyers. We are grateful to them as friends as well as sources. Donald Miller's magnificent *City of the Century: The Epic of Chicago and the Making of America,* published in the midst of our writing process, was particularly useful in providing a historical context for the peculiarities and foibles of our city's fabled past.

A special thanks also to Bob Remer, noted Chicago book collector and publisher of *Chicago Books in Review,* who not only lent one of us an especially valuable out-of-print book, but took over some of her duties on the Review while she was busy writing *The Great Chicago Trivia & Fact Book.*

Several other people worked with us on compiling this book. In particular we want to thank Karen Barham, D. Clancy, Leora Douraghy, Rebecca Fournier, Barbara Hughett, Diane Monk, and two of our offspring—Nellie Goddard and Sam Boyer. We are grateful to them and other members of our families for being patient with our distraction while we worked mightily to meet a very pressing deadline. Thanks also to our publisher Ron Pitkin, who gave us the opportunity to produce one of the first books on the list of his new company, Cumberland House. We had fun writing this, and we hope our readers will find it equally enjoyable.

INTRODUCTION:

The Last Great American City

Consider Chicago.

Consider that in 1833, when Chicago organized itself as a town, it had just over 300 inhabitants. Four years later the town had become a city with a population of 4,170.

There were already 20,000 Chicagoans by 1847, the year the city hosted its first big professional meeting. This was the Rivers and Harbors Convention, and it attracted so many visitors—nearly 20,000—that they almost outnumbered the city's residents.

Consider that by 1860 Chicago's population had swelled to over 100,000 residents, making it one of the largest cities in America. That same year, Chicago hosted its first national political convention, the one that nominated Abraham Lincoln. Ironically, Chicago was home as well to Stephen A. Douglas, the Democratic Party candidate Lincoln would defeat in the general election.

Consider that by 1871, at the time of the Great Chicago Fire, the city had a population of 334,000. The fire did little or nothing to slow the city's growth.

Consider that in 1893 Chicago staged the World's Columbian Exposition and welcomed 26 million people—nearly half the population of the entire United States at that time. By then Chicago itself had 1,250,000 residents, making it one of the biggest cities in the world. Only 60 years earlier it had been little more than a frontier village.

Consider the phenomenon of Chicago.

Henry Adams, grandson of one president and great-grandson of another, came to the exposition in 1893 and remarked, "If one is to consider American thought as a unity, one must begin here." It's still true. Today, Chicago is the planet's twenty-fifth largest city, behind such unexpected places as Lagos, Jakarta, and Mexico City. But it remains the youngest of the world's great cities. Any Chicagoan born before 1913—and there are quite a few—is at least half as young as this city itself.

The Columbian Exposition did much to define Chicago in the eyes of the world. During the boisterous campaign to earn the right to host the exposition, the city's supporters made a great many boasts, which drew a famous quip from a newspaper editor in rival New York who suggested the rest of the country should ignore the claims of that "Windy City." But those who later visited the big show learned that Chicago had earned its bragging rights. Not only had it grown incredibly fast, it had become the center of the continental railroad system, the nation's chief grain and livestock market, and a definitive influence on American architecture, literature, and social welfare.

Between the exposition and the First World War, ideas and machines created in Chicago shaped modern American civilization. Historian Kenan Heise has described this process as "the Chicagoization of America." Then, rather like a vessel that had grown from canoe to ocean liner—too fast for its own good—Chicago seemed to run out of steam. It continued to grow and invent, but at a less-astounding pace, and the lawlessness that had lurked beneath the water line suddenly came up on deck.

In the 1920s Chicago became a city known for political buffoons, bootleggers, and gangland wars. But while the tommy guns barked and the newspaper headlines screamed, Chicago entrepreneurs continued to innovate. Its inventors gave the world the zipper, the window envelope, the car radio, processed cheese, and thousands of other new things that, nowadays, we all take for granted. Chicago social scientists created the settlement house, the juvenile justice system, and the modern concept of social work, while the city became the world's leading center for medical education.

Consider the extraordinary variety of peoples who have made Chicago what it is, for no other city has been such a melting pot. Its first inhabitant was Jean-Baptiste Pointe du Sable, a man of mixed French and Haitian parentage. Over the two centuries wave after wave of immigrants have followed du Sable to this place. They came from Ireland, Sweden, Germany, Bohemia, Greece, Italy, China, and every nation on earth. By 1990 the city had more Poles than Warsaw, more Lithuanians than Vilnius. Of course, people have come here, too, from New England, the Old South, and every corner of America. Among them, we are happy to say, is the high-flying Michael Jordan, who came from North Carolina to become Chicago's best known ambassador.

Consider the words of lawyer and amateur historian Isaac Arnold, who helped found the Chicago Historical Society way back in 1868: "We have boasted long enough of our grain elevators, our railroads, our trade in wheat and lumber, our business palaces; let us now have libraries, galleries of art, scientific museums, noble architecture and public parks ... and a local literature; otherwise there is danger that Chicago will become merely a place where ambitious young men will come to make money and achieve fortune, and then go elsewhere to enjoy it." As if in answer to Arnold, Chicago has become the home of standard-setting orchestras, opera companies, and museums—including the new Museum of Contemporary Art—as well as the Goodman and Steppenwolf theater companies, distinguished university presses, and blues and jazz clubs galore.

And finally, consider that Chicago can claim the world's busiest airport, some of its tallest buildings, its longest open lakeshore, and its second-largest public transit system. All of this may lead visitors to see Chicago as Norman Mailer saw it: "America's last great city." Most of the people fortunate enough to live here call it "America's most livable great city." The authors are pleased to be among the latter, and we hope you will think of Chicago as we do—one great place indeed!

The Great Chicago Trivia & Fact Book is our answer to those who want to learn more about this robust and dynamic city. And have fun doing it. Want to know the name of Chicago's first crooked politician? How many telephone numbers Chicago had in 1886? The average price of a beef steer in 1930? What Clarence Darrow and the *Spoon River Anthology* have in common? Why Bugs Moran hated Valentine's Day? The name of John Dillinger's last movie? Why journalist Ben Hecht was known as the best "picture thief" in the newspaper business? The first player to hit a home run in Comiskey Park? Read on.

The Great
Chicago
Trivia
& Fact
Book

CHAPTER 1

The Good, the Bad, and the Basics

In ancient times, all roads led to Rome; in modern times, all roads lead to Chicago.

D. J. KENNY, 1886

Nobody has ever built a city like this before.

UNKNOWN

Although explorer Louis Jolliet and Father Jacques Marquette were neither the first people to camp alongside the lazy stream that flowed into Lake Michigan, nor perhaps even the first Europeans to visit, they were the first to leave a written record of their stay. Thus the history of Chicago begins in the year of their visit—1673. That spring they left a French fort at the head of Lake Michigan with a crew of five voyageurs to find a great river known as the Mesippi.

They traveled down Green Bay and paddled along the Fox and Wisconsin Rivers into the "father of waters," the Mississippi. They followed that mighty river's course to a point south of where the city of Memphis now stands and then headed north again. A young Native American boy accompanying them suggested they take a shortcut back to Lake Michigan. He directed them eastward up a river we know as the Illinois, then northward up the Des Plaines. Sometime in early September they camped on a narrow ridge between the river and a swamp, then crossed the swamp and came upon a muddy stream that today is known as the Chicago River.

The place at which we entered the lake is a harbor, very convenient for receiving vessels and sheltering them from the wind. The river is wide and deep, abounding in catfish and sturgeon. Game is abundant there; oxen, cows, stags, does and

turkeys were found there in greater numbers than elsewhere. For a distance of
eighty leagues, I did not pass a quarter of an hour without seeing some.

LOUIS JOLLIET

Q: From what direction did these explorers come upon the place where
Chicago was to be built?

A: From the southwest, not from Lake Michigan, as commonly assumed.

Q: The now famous Chicago Portage where they camped is a part of the
Cook County Forest Preserve and is marked by an imposing monument
to the explorers. Where is this located?

A: At Harlem Avenue just north of the Stevenson Expressway. It is possible
to walk along the ridge where they camped, a rise that the astute
observer Jolliet realized was nearly as significant as the portage they had
come upon.

Q: What was so special about this ridge and the muddy swamp below?

A: The ridge, Jolliet realized, was a continental divide. All the water to its
east flowed into the Great Lakes, while the water to its west flowed
toward the Mississippi and the Gulf of Mexico. A canal between the
Chicago and Des Plaines Rivers could become an inland water passage
connecting these two key drainages.

1674

Father Marquette spent a winter camped at what is now the intersection of
Damen Avenue and the river's South Branch. Frustrated that he couldn't convince the French government of its strategic importance, Jolliet never returned
to the area.

1682

French explorer Robert Cavelier, Sieur de LaSalle, visited the "Portage de
Checagou," and he, too, saw its potential. "The boundless regions of the West
must send their products to the East," he predicted. But LaSalle was on his way
to Texas and never returned. He did, however, claim all the land between for
France, naming it Louisiana.

1782

Jean-Baptiste Pointe du Sable built a successful trading post near the mouth
of the river, and in 1800 another French trapper named Jean Lalime purchased
it. Three years later, it was sold again to John Kinzie, a rough living brawler
who knew a good opportunity when he saw it.

Between LaSalle's visit and the establishment of du Sable's trading post, there are no records of people living at or visiting the Chicago area other than the Potawatomis who frequently camped here during the summer. In the Potawatomi language the word *Checagou* means "skunk grass" or "wild onion."

1803

Fort Dearborn was erected on the south bank of the Chicago River to guard a point of entry to the Louisiana Purchase—the same land LaSalle had once claimed for France was now U.S. territory.

Q: After whom was Fort Dearborn named?
A: General Henry Dearborn, secretary of war in the cabinet of President Thomas Jefferson.

Q: The late-nineteenth-century painter James Whistler made his mother famous by painting her. What was the connection between Whistler's father and Chicago?
A: George Washington Whistler, father of painter James Abbott McNeil Whistler, lived at Fort Dearborn as a toddler. His father, Captain John Whistler, was the first army commander at Fort Dearborn.

1810

Helen Hadduck was born at Fort Dearborn. She was the first child born at the settlement since the birth of Eulalia Pointe du Sable in 1796. Later she would marry John DeKoven, a founder of the Northern Trust Company. Social reformer Louise DeKoven Bowen was their granddaughter.

1812

The settlement's relationship with the Potawatomis remained peaceful until British agents began to spread ferment among tribes in the West. Unable to protect the small local civilian population, the U.S. Army told residents to evacuate the fort and head eastward to Indiana. Only about a mile south of the fort, the evacuees were attacked and killed in what is known as the Fort Dearborn Massacre. John Kinzie and his family escaped unharmed, but they didn't return to Chicago until 1816, after a second Fort Dearborn was built.

Q: Where was the fort located?
A: Its boundaries are marked by bronze bars in the sidewalk at Michigan and Wacker. Bas-reliefs on the Michigan Avenue Bridge illustrate aspects of early Chicago history.

Q: How is the site of the massacre marked?

A: A plaque at the intersection of Prairie and 18th Streets marks the approximate location. A monument to the massacre is located nearby in the Prairie Avenue Historic District.

1814

A Baltimore newspaper commented that a canal would make Chicago "the seat of an immense commerce; and a market for the commodities of all regions.... What a route! How stupendous the idea!"

1823

A mineralogist from the University of Pennsylvania who visited Chicago was less impressed: "The village presents no cheering prospect.... it consists of but few huts, inhabited by a miserable race of men, scarcely equal to the Indians from whom they are descended.... As a place of business, it offers no inducement to the settler; for the whole annual shipment of the trade on the lake did not exceed the cargo of five or six schooners.... [The] dangers attending the navigation of the lake, and the scarcity of harbors along the shore, must ever prove a serious obstacle to the increases of the commercial importance of Chicago."

1830

Federal surveyors visited Chicago with the thought of building the canal first envisioned by Jolliet. For some time, a ragtag party of traders and adventurers had been camping on Wolf Point—now the site of the Apparel Center—the only place high enough to keep their sleeping rolls dry. Now they were joined by land speculators. Chicago was born.

> *Buy by the acre, sell by the foot.*
>
> Advice of an early land speculator

1833

A treaty was signed with the Potawatomis that sent them out to Iowa. Chicago organized itself as a town of a few hundred people. Land bought one year would be sold for 100 times that much only a year later.

1834

The Reverend Jeremiah Porter organized Chicago's first church (Presbyterian) and preached its first sermon. That same year, Eliza Chappel opened the community's first public school. A few years later they married, making them Chicago's first power couple.

1836

In an exuberant Fourth of July celebration work began on the Illinois-Michigan Canal. Rather than simply connect the Chicago and Des Plaines Rivers, as was originally envisioned, it headed 90 miles south to the Illinois River at LaSalle. A presiding official enthusiastically predicted that "a hundred years from this time you will have a city of 100,000." He was wrong. It would take Chicago only 25 years to reach a population of 100,000.

Q: Groundbreaking for the canal was held in a small settlement of Irish immigrants called Canalport. A few years later it would become known as Bridgeport. What is the origin of that name?

A: Some clever residents realized that if a bridge over the canal was built too low for loaded barges to pass under it, the goods would have to be unloaded and portaged to the other side. This in turn would provide jobs and money for Bridgeport residents. Here was an early example of the Irish genius for using Chicago politics to their advantage.

1837

Chicago reorganized itself as a city. Its first mayor was William B. Ogden, a recent arrival from upstate New York. Chicago's population had grown tenfold since it had been organized as a town only four years earlier. The first census of Chicago residents counted 1,800 adult males, 845 adult females, 831 children, 1,094 "sailors," and 77 "persons of color" as well as 398 dwellings, 10 taverns, 17 lawyers' offices, and 5 churches. Young women were so scarce in Chicago that it was the custom for eligible bachelors to meet incoming vessels from Detroit or New York "ready to catch the girls as soon as they landed."

1837

Along with the rest of the country, Chicago was caught in the financial panic of 1837, which led to a nationwide depression. Mayor Ogden's steady leadership prevented the city from declaring bankruptcy. Work on the canal stopped, land speculation slowed, and during the next five years Chicago would acquire only about a thousand new residents annually.

No bottom here—the shortest route to China.

A SIGN ON A WAGON ABANDONED IN
ONE OF CHICAGO'S MUDDY STREETS

1839

When the only bridge across the river was swept away in a storm, residents living south of the river objected to spending money to rebuild it. With the support of the mayor, citizens forged a compromise, and a new bridge was built.

Q: To encourage the compromise, North Siders William Ogden and Walter Newberry offered South Side Catholics a deal they couldn't refuse. What was it?

A: Ogden and Newberry donated at State Street and Chicago Avenue land for construction of Holy Name Cathedral.

1844

Work began once more on the canal as the city's population topped 10,000. Most of Chicago's original settlers—after the Potowatomis and the French—were from Vermont and upstate New York, but now up to a third of its citizens were foreign born. A decade later, half of Chicago's 65,000 residents would be from other countries.

Q: What countries contributed to Chicago's early population growth?

A: In 1844 there were 1,056 Chicagoans from Germany, 972 from Ireland, 531 from "Norway" (more likely Sweden, but census takers were apparently unaware of the difference) and 683 "others." This same census also counted 43 lawyers and 28 physicians.

1848

The young city's economy had fully recovered, and Chicago's growth rate surged to at least 2,000 new residents annually.

Q: In 1848 the potato famine began in Ireland, and all but which of the following developments took place in Chicago?

1. The first ocean-going steamer arrived in Chicago's harbor, and the Illinois-Michigan canal opened.
2. The first telegraph message came in from Milwaukee.
3. The first railroad began operation, bringing in a load of wheat from Des Plaines.
4. The Board of Trade opened and began trading futures on grain stored in the city's first elevator.
5. A stockyard opened along Ashland Avenue.
6. The city's first brewery opened along Clybourn Avenue.

7. An ordinance to suppress the playing of keno, a popular form of gambling, was enacted.
8. Senator Stephen A. Douglas, Illinois's first nationally visible politician, moved to Chicago, as did William Bross, who as *Chicago Tribune* publisher would become known as Chicago's first booster.

A: All of these events took place in 1846 except for number 6. Actually, Chicago's first brewery had been established in 1841 by Michael Diversey and William Lill, both of whom have streets named after them.

Q: Chicago's first train, called the *Pioneer,* is still in Chicago. Where is it located?
A: It is in the transportation exhibit at the Museum of Science and Industry.

1849

On March 12 the Chicago River flooded. At 10 A.M. a mass of ice broke loose on the South Branch and, moving downriver, crushed every bridge and dock in its path. All told, four steamers, six steamboats, 24 brigs, 27 canal boats, and two sloops were damaged. The disaster took two lives, a boy killed at the Randolph Street Bridge and a girl killed by a falling topmast.

1854

Chicago adopted its seal and motto: "Urbs in Hortis" or "City in a Garden."

1855

Chicago established itself as the world's leading exporter of grain.

Q: The city's harbor attracted 6,610 ships during 1855. How much had Chicago's harbor traffic increased since 1830?
A: Fewer than a dozen vessels dropped anchor at Chicago in 1830. By 1855, only 25 years later, the city was seeing nearly twice that number of ships every day.

A sluggish, slimy stream, too lazy to clean itself ... better suited to canoes than to sailing ships.
A VISITOR'S COMMENT ABOUT THE RIVER IN 1848

The best harbor on Lake Michigan [but] the worst harbor and smallest river any great commercial city ever lived on.
A VISITOR IN 1858

1856

The Illinois Central Railroad began offering service between Chicago and Cairo, making it the world's longest railroad at the time. The impact of this was immediately felt, not just by Chicago, but by St. Louis, which lost a substantial portion of its river trade to the railroad. Competition was intense among Chicago, Cincinnati (the original porkopolis), and St. Louis, as their relative populations indicate. In 1836 Chicago had a population of 4,000, St. Louis 15,000, and Cincinnati 40,000. By 1870, Chicago's population was 300,000, approximately equal to that of St. Louis. Both had surpassed Cincinnati. By 1890, Chicago had 1,099,850 people, St. Louis 451,770, and Cincinnati only 296,908.

1857

Rush Street's double drawbridge, built on a center pier, opened for traffic. It was the first steel bridge built west of the Alleghenies.

> *These bridges, as is scandalously asserted of certain ladies' tongues, are hung in the middle and play at both ends.*
> A VISITOR COMMENTING ON CHICAGO'S CENTER-PIER BRIDGES

1859

Streetcar service began with the first horse-drawn cars running regularly down State Street.

1860

Chicago had its first major maritime disaster. The *Lady Elgin,* owned by pioneer Gurdon Hubbard, collided with another ship on a windy winter night off Winnetka and sank with a loss of 287 lives.

1860

Although Abraham Lincoln wasn't a Chicagoan, he visited the young city frequently. *Chicago Tribune* editor Joseph Medill engineered Lincoln's nomination by the new Republican Party.

1861

The first Union soldier killed in the Civil War was Captain Elmer Ellsworth, a Chicagoan. He had founded the Zoave Cadets, a flashily uniformed precision drill team. Although at the start of the war Marshall Field was age 26, Philip Danforth Armour, 28, George Pullman, 29, and Potter Palmer, 34, none of these famous men served in the Union military.

1864

A group of city officials objected when asked to raise another 6,000 troops. President Lincoln was not amused.

Gentlemen, after Boston, Chicago has been the chief instrument in bringing this war upon the country.... It is you who are largely responsible for making blood flow as it has. You called for war until we had it. You called for Emancipation, and I have given it to you. Whatever you have asked you have had. Now you come here begging to be let off from the call for men, which I have made to carry out the war you have demanded. You ought to be ashamed of yourselves.... Go home, and raise your 6,000 extra men.
ABRAHAM LINCOLN, 1864

1865

Camp Douglas, the Confederate prisoner-of-war camp on Chicago's South Side, closed down after the war ended. Over 20,000 Southerners had been imprisoned there, and 6,129 of them died.

Q: Where were the dead Confederate prisoners buried?
A: In Oak Woods Cemetery on 67th Street.

1866

The new Chicago water system, designed by the city's brilliant engineer Ellis Chesbrough, opened with an intake crib two miles out in the lake. Although this prevented the river's worst sewage from backing up into the water supply, it didn't completely solve the problem of contamination. Chesbrough was among the first to suggest that the ultimate solution would be to reverse the river's course.

1869

Tunnels were being cut beneath the Chicago River. The first, under Washington Street, opened to traffic on January 1. Two years later another opened under LaSalle Street. The latter tunnel still exists, but is open only to official vehicles.

Q: With so many bridges being built, why were tunnels being constructed under the river?
A: The bridges were closed so often to make way for river traffic that pedestrians and vehicles found them nearly useless.

1871

The Great Chicago Fire devastated the burgeoning city. The blaze left 90,000 people homeless and destroyed 2.7 square miles of homes and businesses, including the entire commercial district.

Q: Devastating though it was, the Great Fire destroyed only around 10 percent of the city's area. What were Chicago's boundaries then?
A: The city stretched north from Pershing Road to Fullerton Avenue and from the lake to Pulaski Avenue on the west.

1871

In the first few months after the fire relief funds poured into the devastated city. Eventually these amounted to $4,820,148, of which $973,897 came from 29 foreign countries. President Ulysses S. Grant sent $1,000 of his own money, while $90 came from citizens of the Dakota Territory.

Nothing of the least consequence to the future of the city perished in the flames. Only buildings and perishable property to be at once replaced.
JOHN S. WRIGHT, FOUNDING EDITOR OF THE *PRAIRIE FARMER*

1879

Kentucky-born Carter Henry Harrison won his first term as Chicago's mayor. Suave and energetic, he kept the immigrant and native populations from major conflict as the city's population burgeoned. Between the fire and the Columbian Exposition, Chicago's population doubled twice, growing from 334,000 to 1,250,000.

Q: What nationality made up the majority of Chicago's population?
A: Germans have always outnumbered all other ethnic groups, and this remains true of the metropolitan area even today.

Q: What percentages of the total population did the immigrant communities represent?
A: The Irish and Germans together composed 40 percent of the population, Scandinavians constituted 10 to 15 percent, and immigrants from other lands—particularly Czechoslovakia, Italy, and Lithuania—made up another 10 percent.

1886

Labor unrest among the city's thousands of factory workers, most of whom were immigrants, led a group of Chicago tycoons to approach Mayor

Harrison and express their concern for the city's safety. At that meeting, Marshall Field began by noting that the group represented "powerful interests" in the city.

> *Mr. Field, any poor man owning a very small cottage as his sole possession has the same interest in Chicago as its richest citizen.*
> MAYOR HARRISON'S RESPONSE TO MARSHALL FIELD

1886

Field and other members of the Commercial Club felt that labor unrest necessitated the presence of federal troops, so they raised money to buy land south of Waukegan and persuaded the federal government to station troops there.

Q: What was the name of the outpost?
A: Upon his death in 1888 the fort was named after Civil War hero General Philip Sheridan, as was the road built to speed soldiers into the city. Sheridan had settled in Chicago shortly before the fire.

Q: What has become of Fort Sheridan?
A: A federal commission suggested that it be closed as superfluous. The land is currently being developed for other uses.

Q: General Sheridan quickly made a name for himself in Chicago. Which one of the following was not among his contributions to the city?

1. During the fire, he ordered buildings on Congress Street near Wabash blown up to prevent the flames from spreading south.
2. He was founder and first president of the Washington Park Racing Club.
3. A statue in his honor was built in Grant Park, which had been named after his Civil War commander.
4. He was a fine dancer and particularly popular with women.

A: Number 3 is incorrect. Sheridan's statue is actually in Lincoln Park near Belmont Avenue. Its sculptor was Gutzon Borglum, who is best known for carving Mount Rushmore.

After the army fort was established, the rival Merchants Club gave land farther north for building a navy base. Although 800 miles from the nearest ocean, Great Lakes Naval Training Station remains the nation's largest naval training facility.

1892

The first elevated rapid-transit line began service between Congress and 39th Streets. During the fair held the following year the first third-rail electric traction system was demonstrated. In a few years, "traction king" Charles Yerkes would have the line extended downtown, giving the Loop its distinctive shape. This elevated train, now called the Green Line, was recently reopened after a complete refurbishment.

1893

At the World's Columbian Exposition a University of Wisconsin historian delivered a famous talk on the importance of the frontier in the American imagination. Called the *Turner Thesis,* it was only one of the fair's countless significant events.

> *The frontier begins with the Indian and the hunter; it goes on to tell of the disintegration of savagery by the entrance of the trader, the pathfinder of civilization … and finally, the manufacturing organization with city and factory system.*
> FREDERICK JACKSON TURNER

Q: Turner's thesis is given less credence today, particularly by another University of Wisconsin historian who nearly 100 years later developed an equally significant thesis concerning Chicago's development. Who is he?

A: William Cronon, whose *Nature's Metropolis: Chicago and the Great West* argues that neither the economy of Chicago nor that of the nation's heartland would have been possible without the other—that they were interdependent.

1897

One of the first industrialists to make use of Fort Sheridan's troops was George Mortimer Pullman, whose ineptness in labor relations led to a strike of his factory's workers during the depression that began right after the fair closed.

> *I shall try to benefit humanity where it is in my power to do so.*
> GEORGE M. PULLMAN

1897

Pullman died and was buried under tons of steel and concrete to prevent his former employees from disinterring his body. Although he left an estate of $21 million, his twin sons were given only $3,000 each. Pullman argued that they hadn't demonstrated much responsibility.

1900

Sanitation and clean drinking water had always been a problem for this city built in a swamp, so after several typhoid fever plagues the Chicago River became the first in the world to flow away from its mouth. The Sanitary and Ship Canal was built to drain the river down to the Mississippi via the Illinois River.

Q: What is the reason for the locks at the river's mouth?
A: They are not intended to keep the river from flowing back into the lake—gravity and the sanitary canal take care of that—but to restrict the flow of water out of Lake Michigan.

1910

The population of Chicago was 2,185,283. By 1880 it had already become the third-largest city in the nation and, by 1890 the second largest, a ranking it would maintain for nearly 100 years.

1915

In one of the world's worst maritime disasters, 812 people were killed when the excursion steamer *Eastland* capsized at its Clark Street berth in the Chicago River. This was nearly three times as many people as perished in the Great Fire and more than half as many as went down with the *Titanic*.

1920

Largely as a result of the demand for labor during the First World War, African-Americans began moving to Chicago. By the war's end they composed about 5 percent of the city's population.

1924

The Volsted Act became law in 1920, and Chicago, which had been a center of agitation for prohibition, became the most vivid example of why it wouldn't work. Nearly 1,000 illegal breweries were soon producing beer in the Little Hell neighborhood, and a master organizer named Johnnie Torrio divided the city into districts, with each of a half dozen gangs controlling one. Within a few years he turned the operation over to his lieutenant, Al Capone, who wanted to establish direct control over the entire metropolitan area.

1925

By 1925 Chicago had more movable bridges than any other city in the world. These consisted of the following: 10 center swing, 24 trunnion bascule, 12 rolling lift, one vertical lift, one Strauss bascule, and three pontoon.

Q: The trunnion bascule bridges, though not invented in Chicago, were developed here. These marvels of engineering are the bridges crossing the main and south branches of the river downtown. What is special about them?

A: The Michigan Avenue Bridge, for example, is a double-leaf, double-decker, trunnion bascule type. It is designed so that a 40-horsepower engine starts the lifting motion, and a counterweight then raises the bridge.

1926

A young pilot named Charles Lindbergh initiated airmail service between Chicago and St. Louis.

1927

Municipal Airport (later named Midway after the World War II U.S. victory in the Pacific) opened near Cicero and 51st Street. It quickly became the nation's busiest airfield. Chicago's first airfield, also the first in the Midwest, had been built near Cicero and 22nd Street in 1910.

1943

On October 17 the first public subway in Chicago opened. Seven years later Chicago's second subway, the Milwaukee-Dearborn line, opened. The Chicago Transit Authority's most recent line, to Midway Airport, opened in 1994.

1949

Chicago, still the railroad capital of the world, retained its role as the world's largest aviation center with the opening of O'Hare Airport. In addition to handling more passengers than any other airport (67 million in 1995), it has the world's largest parking garage.

Q: Who was O'Hare Airport named after?

A: It was named in honor of Edward Henry "Butch" O'Hare, a naval aviator whose heroic action saved his carrier from serious damage; he later lost his life during another World War II battle.

Q: Butch O'Hare's father played a significant role in Capone's conviction for income tax evasion. What was it?

A: A lawyer who managed dog-racing tracks for the mob, O'Hare wanted to go legit so as to not endanger his son's chance to attend Annapolis. When asked to serve as a government informant, he complied. His testimony was crucial in linking Capone with unreported income. In reprisal O'Hare was murdered gangland style while his son was learning to fly.

Q: Travelers in and out of O'Hare Field see signs for Bessie Coleman Drive. Whom is it named for?

A: The Chicagoan who in 1921 became the first black woman in America to earn a pilot's license. Because no U.S. airport would take her on as a student, she had to go to France to learn to fly. She died in a 1926 airplane accident.

1950

Chicago's population peaked at 3,618,500. Within 30 years it had declined to just over three million. By 1990 it had fallen to 2,783,726.

Q: Chicago still has the longest continuous street of any city in the United States. What is it?

A: It is Western Avenue, running the entire north-south length of the city, a distance of 24.5 miles. At 92nd Street, Western Avenue passes over the highest elevation in the city, 683 feet.

1979

In the worst aviation disaster in U.S. history, an American Airlines DC-10 crashed shortly after taking off at O'Hare Airport, killing all 275 people aboard.

1992

In April Chicago's turn-of-the-century freight tunnel system flooded when new pilings were being driven into the Chicago River bed. Dozens of downtown buildings were flooded, resulting in millions of dollars worth of damage, and Chicagoans became aware of yet one more of the city's wonders they hadn't known existed.

CHAPTER 2

City on the Make

This will be the gate of empire, this the seat of commerce. Everything invites to action. The typical man who will grow up here must be an enterprising man. Each day as he rises, he will exclaim, "I act, I move, I push," and there will be spread before him a boundless horizon.

ROBERT CAVELIER, SIEUR DE LASALLE, UPON PASSING THROUGH "LE PORTAGE DE CHECAGOU" IN THE WINTER OF 1682

It is the only great city in the world to which all its citizens have come for the one common, avowed object of making money.

HENRY BLAKE FULLER, *THE CLIFF DWELLERS,* 1893

Chicago is, above all else, a business town. Its history and culture are permeated with stories of people seeking fame and fortune on the shores of Lake Michigan.

What made those fortunes possible was a growth so rapid as to be beyond grasp today. In 1850 Chicago was a modest port and railroad center with some 30,000 inhabitants. When it hosted the World's Columbian Exposition in 1893, Chicago's population had grown to 1,100,000—a 3,700 percent increase in less than 50 years!

Chicago accomplished this feat by riding the wave of the Industrial Revolution, and creating wealth on a colossal scale. Hundreds of new American industries—from reapers to railroads, mail-order merchandising to appliance manufacturing, bowling balls to jukeboxes, cattle processing to processed cheese—came to life in boomtown Chicago.

Who created the wealth? Settlers from New York and New England at first, to be followed in short order by immigrants from Ireland, Germany, Scandinavia, Poland, Italy, and a dozen other countries. Around World War I the great migration of African-Americans from the Old South began, and brought with it whole new enterprises in banking, publishing, cosmetics, and music.

Fittingly enough, the story of Chicago as a business center begins with the founding of a business by a man of mixed race and background. The first recorded structure in Chicago history was a general store opened by Jean-Baptiste Pointe du Sable, a Haitian with French blood, sometime around 1780.

1800

Du Sable sold his business near the mouth of the Chicago River to another Frenchman named Jean Lalime.

Q: Du Sable's establishment was the site for which of the following Chicago firsts?

1. The first election.
2. The first court.
3. The first post office.
4. The first marriage.

A: All of the above.

1804

Du Sable's trading post was sold again, this time to John Kinzie, a trader and friend of the Potawatomi population. After the Fort Dearborn massacre Kinzie moved his family to Michigan. He returned in 1816 and established himself as a deal-maker and less-than-honest trader.

1826

Mark Beaubien, a fiddle-playing French Canadian with a wild streak, arrived in Chicago to visit his brother Jean-Baptiste. He decided to stay and opened a popular tavern and hotel called the Sauganash.

Q: Sauganash today is the name of a residential district favored by bureaucrats and prosperous Irish families (former Mayor Jane Byrne grew up there). Nearby Caldwell Woods got its name from the same source as the neighborhood it borders. Explain the connection.

A: Billy Caldwell, an early settler of Irish and Mohawk parentage, was known to the Potawatomi who had adopted him as Sauganash, or "the white man." Caldwell was awarded 1,600 acres of land when the Peace Treaty of 1829 was signed. Known today as Caldwell Woods, the land is located in the Forest Preserve District's holdings near Sauganash.

1830

Federal canal surveyors arrived, and Chicago's land rush began when Easterners began buying on speculation. In 1833 some early investors sent William B. Ogden to Chicago to check on their property, and the city gained both an ardent booster and a vital link to New York money.

1831

In an effort to curb rampant speculation Cook County enacted its first price controls. They included: breakfast or supper, 25 cents; dinner, 37.5 cents; cider and beer, 6.25 cents per pint; feed for horses, 25 cents; a night's lodging for a horse, 50 cents; a nights lodging for a man 12.5 cents.

1831

The first permanent post office opened in Chicago.

1833

Despite the price controls enacted two years earlier, short supplies and strong demand sent prices soaring once again. Flour sold for $20 a barrel, and butter and potatoes, according to one contemporary source, "were only a memory."

1834

By the next year supply and demand had stabilized. For those who had survived, potatoes could be had for $1.25 per bushel.

1834

A "bull" plow with a wooden mold board—the business end of a plow—became the first farm implement to be manufactured in Chicago, and George W. Dole opened a slaughterhouse and made the first shipment of beef from Chicago—287 barrels. Chicago's two most famous industries had been born.

1836

The rapid influx of new settlers, along with the plans for a canal to link Chicago with downstate Illinois and the Mississippi River valley, set off unrestrained land speculation. Gurdon S. Hubbard, who had purchased two lots for less than $80 in 1831, was paid $80,000 for them a mere five years later.

Q: Gurdon Hubbard is remembered for all but which of the following?

1. Native Americans called him Papamatabe, or Swift Walker, out of respect for his strength and endurance.

2. He was the city's first meatpacker and partner in the first real hotel.

3. He was married to Juliette A. Magill, Chicago's first novelist.

4. He owned the *Lady Elgin,* which went down in a Lake Michigan storm on November 8, 1860, resulting in 297 deaths.

5. He bought the first Chicago fire engine.

6. He was instrumental in building the Illinois-Michigan canal.

A: Number 3. Juliette A. Magill, author of *Wau-Bun: Early Days of the Northwest,* was married to John Harris Kinzie, son of the pioneer John Kinzie. The first two streets north of the Chicago River were named for Kinzie and Hubbard, respectively.

1835

The English writer Harriet Martineau visited Chicago as a guest of William Ogden and, appalled by all the land trading and streets full of men offering bargains, predicted the end of "this money-making evil" and a quick bursting of the bubble. Her prediction, alas, proved all too true in the panic of 1837.

It seems as if, on all hands, people came here merely to trade, to make money, and not to live.

HARRIET MARTINEAU

1836

In the burgeoning city carpenters and joiners made $2.50 per day, common laborers $1.50 to $2.00, and bricklayers and masons $3.00. *The Chicago Democrat,* the city's first newspaper, reported that such wages were "most enormously high."

Q: The owner of the *Chicago Democrat* would, 20 years later, become mayor of the city. He was known for his great height. What was his name?

A: John Wentworth.

1837

The first Sherman House Hotel was built at Randolph and Clark.

Q: Who was the hotel named after, and what business was he in?

A: Francis C. Sherman, who owned a brick factory. He also served two terms as mayor between 1841-42 and 1862-65.

Q: The first Sherman House was designed by architect William Boyington. What other famous Chicago landmark did he design?

A: The Water Tower.

1839

The firm of Newberry and Dole shipped 1,678 bushels of wheat up Lake Michigan on the ship Osceola, marking the beginning of Chicago's leading role in grain export trade.

Q: What famous Chicago institution owes its existence to the business success of Newberry and Dole?
A: The Newberry Library, one of the world's leading rare book collections, was created in 1877 under the will of Walter Loomis Newberry.

1841

The first issue of the *Prairie Farmer* appeared. A product of the Union Agricultural Society and its visionary editor, John S. Wright, it was the first periodical to be published in Chicago.

1841

The first book to be printed in Chicago appeared that same year: *Reports of Supreme Court Decisions,* published by J. Young Scammon and Stephen F. Gale.

1841

A soap and candle factory run by Charles Cleaver was declared a nuisance by the Board of Health. Cleaver, an English immigrant, had built his factory in an area that came to be called Cleaverville, Chicago's first suburb.

Q: Where was it located?
A: Between 37th and 39th Streets, near Ellis Avenue. Cleaver also built himself an imposing house in the same district. He named it Oakwood Hall, which gave its name to the neighborhood now known as Oakwood.

1842

A. B. Wheeler began manufacturing Habana Princepe and Cuba cigars, marketing them with the exclusive slogan, "Puff Dull Care Away." Chicago's role as a center of advertising had begun.

1843

Alexander Clybourn, Chicago's first constable, and Gurdon Hubbard slaughtered the first cattle to be sent from Chicago to markets in the East.

Q: How do Chicagoans know Clybourn's name today?
A: Clybourn Avenue, a major street heading northwest out of the Loop, was named after him.

1844

After only one year, Gurdon Hubbard, the largest meatpacker in town, was slaughtering 300 to 400 hogs per day.

1844

Cyrus H. McCormick, whose father had invented the reaper, noted the large number of orders coming from Chicago, so he came West to see what the excitement was all about. In the process he hired a young circuit lawyer named Abraham Lincoln to represent him in a legal battle over patent violations.

Q: Where did McCormick manufacture his reapers?
A: Under the name of McCormick and Gray, he built his reaper factory on the north bank of the Chicago River early in 1847. By summer's end he had already sold 200 reapers at $120 each.

Q: What did a reaper do, and why was it so important to the development of the Midwest?
A: It cut and gathered hay five times faster than by hand, making large-scale agriculture feasible.

1847

The *Chicago Tribune,* later to be owned by McCormick heirs, was founded at Lake and LaSalle Streets.

1847

Chicago hosted its first convention, the River and Harbor Convention. Horace Greeley, known later as publisher of the *New York Tribune* and for his famous advice to "Go West, young man," was among the 20,000 visitors, including 300 delegates from 18 states, who attended. Most arrived by lake vessels as no railroad had yet reached the city. The number of visitors nearly equaled the city's population at the time.

1848

The first cattle yards were opened at Bull's Head, where Madison Street meets Ashland and Ogden Avenues. A balloon-frame tavern of the same name was erected there as well and remained standing for over a half century.

Q: What city park is located near this intersection now, and how did it get its name?

A: It is Union Park, so named because of the many labor union headquarters located along Ashland Avenue.

1848

The Chicago area's first railroad, the Galena and Chicago Union, headed by William Ogden, completed its first 10-mile run on November 20, 1848, between the city and the Des Plaines River. It would evolve over time into the Chicago & North Western Railroad.

1849

The Chicago Gas Light & Coke Company was "chartered in perpetuity." Within a year—on September 5, 1850—Chicago had its first gas lights.

1851

Chicago had 14 weekly, six daily, and four monthly papers. The dailies were the *Democrat, Advertiser, Argus, Tribune, Staats Zeitung,* and *Journal.*

1852

Chicago corn buyers established the official weight of a bushel of corn at 56 pounds.

Q: By 1852 how many years had passed since the city's incorporation?
A: Fifteen.

1853

A young man named Frank Parmalee saw that money could be made transferring railroad passengers and their effects from station to station or hotel. From this observation grew the Parmalee Transfer Company. His smartly dressed drivers were the first thing most arriving passengers saw.

Q: How were hogs and human passengers treated differently by the railroads?
A: Hogs rode on through trains directly to their unhappy destinations.
  People, on the other hand, had to stay in town and catch a meal or two because all passenger routes terminated in Chicago.

1853

Anthony Trollope, the noted English novelist, visited Chicago and stayed at the Briggs House on the corner of Randolph and Wells. He was unimpressed. "There were pipes without end for cold water, which ran hot, and for hot water, which would not run at all," he said.

1854

An Ohio newspaperman named Joseph Medill arrived in Chicago and acquired an interest in the *Chicago Tribune*. Six years later his fervent support would secure the Republican presidential nomination for Abraham Lincoln.

Q: Medill was the founder of a newspaper dynasty. What other newspapers did his descendants own?

A: His grandson Robert McCormick ran the *Tribune* from 1911 until his death in 1955. Another grandson, Joseph Medill Patterson, moved east in 1921 to establish the *New York Daily News*. Patterson's sister, Eleanor "Cissy" Patterson, edited the *Washington, D.C., Herald* after buying it from William Randolph Hearst.

1855

A retail store known as Mandel Brothers was opened at the corner of Clark and Van Buren by three brothers from Germany: Simon, Leon, and Emmanuel Mandel.

Q: In 1912 the Mandel brothers opened a store on State Street, and the building still stands. What stores have occupied it over time?

A: Mandel Brothers expanded the building to Wabash Avenue, and it eventually became a Wieboldt's store. In 1990 Filene's Basement opened its first Chicago store there, and T. J. Maxx moved in on the second floor.

1855

Chicago became the national center for the lumber trade. Boats bearing lumber from Wisconsin and Michigan passed ships loaded with grain heading north and east as far as Buffalo.

Q: Why was this maritime *pas de deux* so central to Chicago's rapid growth?

A: Lumber cut and sawed from Michigan and Wisconsin forests became, via the railroads, barns and houses for farmers on the plains who in turn produced the grain and cattle processed in and shipped from Chicago.

Nature built Chicago through her artificer, Man.

JOHN M. BINCKLEY

1855

The Crane Company was established in a machine shop the size of a modern two-car garage. A century later it would occupy 72 acres of floor space on the city's South Side and be the world's largest manufacturer of valves and fittings. It also produced plumbing fixtures, radiators, and kitchen cabinets.

Q: What institution is named after Crane, and what other institution did it spawn?

A: Crane Technical High School on the West Side was also the first home of Malcolm X Community College.

1856

A young New Englander arrived in Chicago from Pittsfield, Massachusetts, and became a clerk at Cooley, Wadsworth and Company. His name was Marshall Field, and he was determined to make good.

Give the lady what she wants.
MARSHALL FIELD, VOICING THE MOTTO OF HIS DEPARTMENT STORE

He had the best financial mind I'd ever seen.
FINANCIER J. P. MORGAN DESCRIBING MARSHALL FIELD,
WHOM HE'D KNOWN IN PITTSFIELD

1856

More than 21 million bushels of grain were shipped from Chicago, three times the amount shipped only three years earlier. Within a few years Chicago's 12 grain elevators could receive and ship 500,000 bushels of grain every 10 hours.

Q: What nickname was given to the grain as it flowed like water into grain elevators?

A: Liquid Gold. The name is immortalized in elevator panels in the Board of Trade Building at LaSalle and Jackson.

1865

George Pullman's first sleeping coach, the *Pioneer,* carried Abraham Lincoln's body back from Washington. Two years later Pullman's Palace Car Company was chartered.

Q: Lincoln's funeral procession was not the last link between the late President's family and the company Pullman founded. Name the other.

A: Lincoln's son Robert later served as president and chairman of the board of the Pullman Palace Car Company.

1865

The Union Stock Yard and Transit Company of Chicago opened for business on Christmas Day. Its three miles of watering troughs used 500,000 gallons of water daily. Within a few years the yard sold cow manure for 10 cents a wagon—less than the cost of having it shoveled up.

Q: What is the significance of the words "transit company" in the stockyard company's name?

A: The stockyards were actually created by the railroad companies whose business it was to bring live animals into Chicago and to carry the dressed meat out.

1865

Philip Danforth Armour, having panned for gold in California and sold hides in Minnesota, had arrived during the Civil War. Now he began to build the foundation for his meatpacking empire.

Most people talk too much. Most of my success has been due to keeping my mouth shut.... I have no other interest in life but my business.... I do not love the money; what I do love is the getting of it, the making it.
                                        PHILIP DANFORTH ARMOUR

1868

Field, Leiter and Company opened at the corner of State and Washington. The firm had been started a few years earlier by Field, Potter Palmer, and Levi Leiter, but Palmer had departed to pursue other interests.

Q: What business did Palmer go into?

A: Realizing that the east-west streets in downtown Chicago were limited by the lake and the river, Palmer determined that future growth had to come along a north-south axis, so he left retailing to develop real estate on State Street.

1870

The Sturgis & Buckingham grain elevator inside the Illinois Central yards near the mouth of the Chicago River could store three million bushels at one time.

I am satisfied that there is no institution in the State of Illinois that can pile up money like the elevators in Chicago.
                        A DELEGATE TO THE ILLINOIS CONSTITUTIONAL CONVENTION IN 1877

1871

The day after the Great Fire, the *Chicago Journal* put out the first post-fire newspaper. Though it measured only four by six inches and was printed on one side, it was there!

We have lost money, but we have saved life, health, vigor and industry.... Let the Watchword henceforth be: Chicago Shall Rise Again!
JOSEPH MEDILL IN A *CHICAGO TRIBUNE* EDITORIAL THREE DAYS AFTER THE FIRE

1871

Marshall Field and Levi Leiter, whose State Street store had opened only three years earlier, saved some $600,000 worth of goods and hauled it to a South Side stable that temporarily became their new store.

1871

Elisha Gray and Enus Barton, operators of a small telegraph company in Cleveland, moved to Chicago. Their ability to reestablish fledgling telegraph service immediately enabled Joseph Medill to order a new printing press from Cincinnati the day after the fire.

Q: What company did Gray and Barton go on to found?
A: Western Electric, which until the 1960s manufactured most of the nation's telephones from its Hawthone Works plant on Cicero Avenue.

1871

In November Joseph Medill was elected mayor of Chicago on the Fireproof Ticket. He served less than two years before ill health and the enmity of many citizens forced him to resign.

Q: What were Medill's political views?
A: In common with many of the Protestant elite, he hated Catholics and Negroes, was virulently opposed to gambling and drinking, and believed that labor organizers were vermin to be exterminated.

A little strychnine or arsenic should be used to flavor the food of striking workers. This produces death within a comparatively short time, is a warning to other tramps to keep out of the neighborhood, puts the Coroner in a good humor, and saves one's chickens and other portable property from constant depredation.
JOSEPH MEDILL IN A *TRIBUNE* EDITORIAL

1872

The post-fire Palmer House claimed to be the world's first fireproof hotel and the first equipped with electricity, telephones, and elevators.

1872

A. Montgomery Ward, who had worked as a clerk at Field & Leiters store upon his arrival in Chicago, opened a mail-order dry goods store on Clark Street.

Q: Ward is known for many retailing innovations, including selling directly to farmers via the mail, but what was his most lasting legacy for the people of Chicago?
A: At the turn of the century Ward waged a one-man campaign to protect the lakefront from commercial development.

Forever open, clear and free of any Buildings, or Other Obstruction Whatsoever.
WARD'S CREDO FOR PRESERVING THE LAKE MICHIGAN SHORELINE,
TAKEN FROM A LEGEND ON THE 1836 PLAT OF CHICAGO

Q: What structure symbolized Montgomery Ward and Company?
A: Called the "Spirit of Progress," it is a statue of a young girl. Though its origins are obscure, it stands today at the top of the company's warehouse at Chicago Avenue and the river, where it can be seen from blocks away.

1878

On June 26 the first telephone office opened in Chicago, barely a year after Alexander Graham Bell invented the device.

1879

Even the Great Fire couldn't destroy Chicago's lumber trade. In 1867 Chicago's 100 lumber yards had just under half a billion feet in stock. By 1879 they were selling three times that much lumber every year.

Q: What families noted for philanthropy made their fortunes in the lumber business, and what did they endow?
A: The Ryersons, better known for their role at Inland Steel, were (and remain) major benefactors of the Art Institute. The Goodmans donated the Goodman Theater to the same institution, and the Ferguson family established a fund there to underwrite public sculptures.

1880s

Chicagoan John Gates once put enough money on the horse Royal Flush in an English horse race to win over $1 million for that one wager—earning himself the sobriquet, "Bet a Million" Gates.

Q: How did Gates make his money, and who was his chief competitor?
A: He made it selling barbed wire, one of the key inventions in settling the plains because it allowed ranchers to fence in their livestock at small expense. Joseph F. Glidden of DeKalb is generally credited with inventing barbed wire, but it was not until 1892 that the Supreme Court resolved the patent claims of many manufacturers—including Gates—in Glidden's favor.

1881

Field & Leiter turned a profit of $2 million. Marshall Field bought out his partner and changed the name to Marshall Field & Company.

Q: What happened to Levi Leiter after Marshall Field bought him out?
A: He left Chicago and the retailing business to live in Washington, D.C., where his wife became a social leader. One of their daughters became Lady Curzon by marrying an English lord who eventually became Viceroy of India.

Q: What retail innovator convinced Marshall Field to open a tearoom in his store, converting it from a simple dry goods store to the full-fledged department store we know today, and then went on to establish a famous department store in London that still bears his name?
A: Harry Gordon Selfridge.

> *This is a dry goods store; we don't feed people here.*
> MARSHALL FIELD UPON FIRST HEARING SELFRIDGE'S SUGGESTION

1882

Chicago's 200 job and book printers included such famous names as R. R. Donnelley, Rand McNally & Company, and the W. F. Hall Printing Company.

Q: Most of these companies were located in a certain part of Chicago. Where was it, and what is it called today?
A: Printers constructed buildings sturdy enough to withstand the vibration of clanking presses on South Dearborn Street. Today the buildings have been redeveloped into apartments known as Printers Row.

1884

Albert Blake Dick founded the A. B. Dick Addressograph Multigraph Company to produce office machinery.

Q: What need did Dick see, and what did he invent to address it?
A: He saw that lumber dealers needed to reproduce price lists for their customers, so he invented the mimeograph.

1885

Swift & Company used 450,000 tons of ice every year for shipping meat, the result of Gustavus F. Swift's insight that the real importance of refrigerator cars was that they enabled meatpacking houses to operate year round. He was also the first packer to transform beef byproducts into such highly profitable items as margarine, glue, soap, and fertilizer.

Q: Gustavus Swift claimed he sold all but what part of the pig?
A: The squeal.

1885

On April 30 the Board of Trade opened at Jackson and LaSalle Streets. In one of Chicago's first significant labor actions, 2,000 workers protested the opening. One of their demands was an eight-hour workday, which they believed would create more jobs.

> *How long will you sit down to fifteen-cent meals when those fellows inside are sitting down to a banquet at twenty dollars a plate?*
>
> A PROTESTER

1885

The first Chicago telephone book had 291 listings. It was printed by R. R. Donnelley in 1886 for the Chicago Telephone Company, predecessor of Illinois Bell.

1887

A young watch salesman from Minnesota named Richard Sears arrived in Chicago. Needing a watchmaker, he ran a newspaper ad that was answered by a Hoosier named Alvah Roebuck. Together, they established what became one of America's largest businesses.

Q: Sears Roebuck & Company's success was founded on farmers and railroads. How did pocket watches bring the two together?

A: Farmers needed accurate timepieces to gauge the arrival of trains that would transport their grain. Indeed, railroad officials had met in Chicago in 1883 to establish the national time zone system that is still intact today.

Q: Name another Chicago company that owes its origins to time and the railroads.

A: Rand McNally, the world's largest mapmaker, originally printed train schedules.

1889

Chicagoans Arthur and Charles Libby, with their friend Archibald MacNeil, developed a method of canning corned beef in their plant at 16th and State, thus starting the packaged foods business that still bears their name today.

1893

The Columbian Exposition opened in May, and over 26 million people paid admission to see it.

For the last half century [the Midwest] has furnished the cow and the grass and the corn, and New York has done the milking. This empire now desires to do the milking herself, and by the noise from New York, I should judge that they realize there that the weaning time has come.
                    REPRESENTATIVE ABNER TAYLOR OF ILLINOIS DURING THE DEBATE
                            IN CONGRESS OVER WHERE TO LOCATE THE 1893 FAIR

Chicago was the first expression of American thought as a unity; one must start there.
                    HENRY ADAMS, UPON SEEING THE COLUMBIAN EXPOSITION

Q: What was the population of Chicago at the time of the 1893 fair? Of the country?

A: Chicago's population was 1,250,000. The entire United States had 63 million people.

Q: What snack food, invented by a popcorn vendor named F. W. Rueckheim, was first sold at the World's Columbian Exposition?

A: Cracker Jack.

Q: What invention that revolutionized publishing was first exhibited at the World's Columbian Exposition?
A: The linotype machine.

1894

The Pullman Strike of 1894 was nicknamed "The Debs Rebellion" after Eugene Debs, who acted as the American Railway Union's field commander. Federal troops were ordered in, the first time this had been done during a labor action.

Q: Which union was one of the first to be organized around an entire industry rather than individual crafts?
A: The American Railway Workers Union, of which Eugene Debs later became president.

1895

Chicago had 276 furniture manufacturing companies employing over 28,000 workers.

1896

The zipper was invented and patented in Chicago by Whitcomb L. Judson, who called it the "hookless fastener."

1900

The average price of a beef steer was $5.15. It rose to $6.80 in 1910 and to $13.30 by 1920. By 1930, however, in the wake of the depression, the average price had fallen to $11.05.

1902

The window envelope was invented by Chicagoan Americus F. Callahan, who called the window an "outlook."

1903

Ontario-born James L. Kraft spent $65 to buy a horse and wagon with which he distributed cheese from the South Water Street Market to retail grocers throughout Chicago. By 1929 the Kraft brand was established throughout the world, and more than 50 subsidiaries were operating in Canada, Australia, England, and Holland.

Q: What technological breakthrough did Kraft make in 1916 that revolutionized the cheese business?

A: The pasteurization of cheese for canning, assuring a long shelf life without refrigeration. During World War I the United States government ordered more than six million tons of Kraft processed cheese to feed its soldiers on the front.

In those days, people didn't care much for cheese.
JAMES L. KRAFT, OF HIS EARLY YEARS IN BUSINESS, JUST BEFORE HE
BEGAN PEDDLING HIS PASTEURIZED, PROCESSED VARIETY

1904

The Chicago Association of Commerce and Industry was established. John G. Shedd, president of Marshall Field & Company, was named its first president.

1906

Upon the death of Marshall Field, the stores along State Street closed on the day of his funeral in respect to his memory.

The sun never sets on Marshall Field's.
JOHN G. SHEDD, PRESIDENT OF MARSHALL FIELD & COMPANY

Q: In 1930 the Shedd Aquarium in Grant Park, which bears John Shedd's name, opened. Fortunes made in the merchandising business were responsible for what other Chicago museums?

A: The Field Museum was endowed by Marshall Field and was run for 60 years by his nephew, Stanley. Sears Roebuck money was responsible for two Chicago museums: the Museum of Science & Industry, funded by Julius Rosenwald, the man who made Sears into a retailing giant, and the Adler Planetarium, endowed by a Sears executive who was also Rosenwald's brother-in-law.

1909

William A. Wieboldt parted with tradition and started establishing a chain of stores in the neighborhoods rather than downtown, opening his first store at Lincoln and Belmont.

My heart is in the neighborhood store. Then I'm part of the community.
WILLIAM A. WIEBOLDT

1911

With the presence of Hart, Schaffner & Marx, Kuppenheimer & Company, and other clothing manufacturers, Chicago produced more men's suits than any other city in the country.

Q: What marketing innovation helped Chicago companies sell more suits?
A: Realizing that pants wore out faster than jackets, Chicago manufacturers started making the two-pant suit.

Q: The Chicago garment industry was shut down for sixteen weeks until garment workers union leader Sidney Hillman got the companies to recognize what principle of labor-management relations?
A: The arbitration of grievances.

1912

Two Polish-born brothers, Nathan and Maurice Goldblatt, opened a store at 1617 W. Chicago Avenue, adopting the slogan "America's Fastest Growing Department Stores."

1912

William Wrigley Jr. moved his rapidly growing chewing gum company to the new Central Manufacturing District (CMD) site on Ashland and 35th Streets. An innovative businessman, his company was one of the first in Chicago to advertise extensively on billboards and streetcars, to give employees Saturdays off, and to provide life insurance for them.

> *Tell 'em quick and tell 'em often.... Anyone can make gum, selling it is the problem.*
> WILLIAM WRIGLEY JR., ON THE IMPORTANCE OF ADVERTISING

1913

A Northwestern University professor and his partner opened Andersen, DeLaney & Co. to offer outside accounting services to companies. Today, Arthur Andersen & Co. is one of the largest accounting firms in the world.

> *Think straight—talk straight.*
> ARTHUR ANDERSEN

1915

A former West Side boxer named John Hertz started a fleet of taxicabs, which he painted yellow to distinguish them from those of his competition. The color inspired the name of the fleet—Yellow Cabs.

Q: What other automobile business did the Yellow Cab founder start?
A: The car-rental business, which Hertz started in Chicago in 1923. He later sold his company to General Motors and moved on to other ventures.

Q: Which of the other "big five" rent-a-car companies is still based in Chicago?
A: Budget Rent-a-Car, which in the late 1980s moved to west suburban Lisle from its North Michigan Avenue location.

1920

Chicago's total labor force numbered 1,250,000, of whom 250,000 were women.

1923

Chicago had the following agricultural and food processing businesses:

- 50 slaughterhouses with 30,382 employees
- 38 pickle & jelly plants with 1,307 employees
- 32 ice cream plants with 666 employees
- 5 flour & milling plants with 248 employees
- 26 flavor extract plants with 223 employees
- 214 tobacco plants with 2,226 employees
- 35 coffee & spice plants with 916 employees
- 4 fish processing & canning plants with 17 employees
- 9 butter plants with 159 employees
- 13 flavor syrup plants with 115 employees
- 1,052 bread and baking plants with 9,926 employees
- 109 beverage plants with 1,119 employees
- 43 sausage plants (not meatpacking) with 1,142 employees

1923

Chicago distributed more butter than any other city, a total of 446 million pounds annually, exceeding the annual output of New York, Philadelphia, and Boston combined.

1923

Chicago's meatpacking industry had been established for 60 years, and some of its business had already been moved to such cities as Omaha and Sioux City. Nonetheless, in this one year 2,144,654 cattle, 744,952 calves, 8,099,361 hogs, and 2,811,540 sheep and lambs died in Chicago slaughterhouses.

1924

Oscar F. Mayer put packaged sliced bacon on the market, one of his many marketing innovations. A few years later, his became one of the first companies to adopt brand identification, wrapping every fourth wiener in a yellow paper ring.

Q: What character and vehicle did his company use to travel around promoting its product? When were they first introduced?
A: Little Oscar and the Weinermobile first appeared in 1936.

1927

The average weekly wage in Chicago was $15.43.

1929

Chicago utility mogul Samuel Insull's empire included Commonwealth Edison, Peoples Gas, and the elevated railroads and interurbans that connected Chicago with its growing suburbs. The stock market crash brought down Insull's empire, and thousands lost their investments in his firms. Accused of running a giant pyramid scheme, Insull fled to Europe to avoid prosecution. After his return in 1934, however, he was tried and acquitted three times for fraud and embezzlement.

Q: What noted Chicago building did Insull have built, and for what is it used today?
A: The Civic Opera House building at 20 North Wacker Drive was completed just before the 1929 crash. It combines offices with a 3,500-seat opera house and a 900-seat theater. As with its counterpart, the Auditorium Building, the commercial spaces were designed to subsidize the theaters. Today, it is the home of the Lyric Opera of Chicago.

Q: Insull's opera house inspired what famous movie?
A: Orson Welles borrowed Insull's idea for his 1939 classic, *Citizen Kane*.

Samuel Insull died in 1938 of a heart attack in a Paris metro station. His body was reportedly identified through the *SI* embroidered on the French cuffs of his shirt.

1930

The pinball machine was invented in Chicago. A ten-balls-for-a-nickel device, originally called the Whoopee Game, was put on the market by In & Outdoor Games Company in 1930.

1930

The Hostess Twinkie was invented in Schiller Park by James Dewar, manager of Continental Baking Company's Hostess Bakery.

1935

Leo Burnett opened his advertising agency. Told he would be out "selling apples" within the year, Burnett placed large bowls of apples around his office for employees to munch on, a practice that continues to this day.

Q: Name several well-known characters in advertising created by the Leo Burnett Agency.

A: Charlie the Tuna, the Pillsbury Doughboy, the Jolly Green Giant, the Harris Lion, the Marlboro Man, Tony the Tiger, Morris the Cat, the Man from Glad, the Keebler Elves.

I expect to shave regularly and to remain fully active within the outer limits of my new status until senility clearly makes me either an old nuisance or a bench warmer.

LEO BURNETT, UPON RETIRING FROM ACTIVE MANAGEMENT
OF THE COMPANY HE FOUNDED

1937

Meatpacking, with a value of $2,391,089,954, was the second-largest industry in the United States, behind motor vehicles. Illinois was ranked number one. Its 79 meatpacking plants accounted for 21 percent of the total, more than twice that of Iowa, which was ranked number two.

1937

Steelmaking had been a major Chicago industry since the turn of the century, and the steelworkers were a major labor presence. On May 30, 10 people were shot and killed during the Republic Steel strike when a rock was thrown and police opened fire. Newsreels of the incident were suppressed because they showed police firing without warning. Many of the killed and wounded were shot in the back as they tried to flee. Police Commissioner James P. Allman was suspected of closeting the films, which were finally shown before a U.S. Senate committee investigating the incident.

1937

The average head of beef cattle weighed 899 pounds and yielded 470 pounds of meat.

1940

The establishment of a special labor detail in the Chicago Police Department encouraged workers to avoid violence and bloodshed during labor strikes. The detail set a precedent that attracted national attention.

1942

Foote, Cone & Belding was formed, with Chicagoan Fairfax M. Cone as chairman. A man of refined taste, Cone refused to accept political advertising of any kind and denounced billboards as destructive of the natural landscape.

Q: Name three famous tag lines created by Foote, Cone & Belding.
A: "Only her hairdresser knows for sure" (Clairol), "Aren't you glad you use Dial? Don't you wish everyone did?" (Dial soap), "When you care enough to send the very best" (Hallmark Greeting Cards), "The quality goes in before the name goes on" (Zenith), and "You'll wonder where the yellow went" (Pepsodent).

1945

Evergreen Plaza, developed by real estate tycoon Arthur Rubloff, was one of the country's first enclosed shopping malls.

Q: Which phrase for describing the posh district north of the river was Chicago real estate developer Arthur Rubloff credited with coining?
A: "Magnificent Mile."

1951

A piece of backyard equipment as essential as the lawn chair was invented in Palatine by a suburbanite Chicagoan who didn't like the then popular method of barbecuing, so he devised a grill more to his liking at the plant where he worked.

Q: What was his name, and how did the grill get its name?
A: George Stephens was an employee of the Weber Brother Metal Works, where he fabricated the prototype grill.

1954

Since the 1880s iron ore had been shipped from the Mesabi Range in Minnesota to steel centers on the Great Lakes. With the three largest steel mills in the country—U.S. Steel's Gary Works and South Works, and Inland Steel—

Chicago became the largest producer of steel in the world, surpassing Pittsburgh for the first time.

Q: Every day nearly 100,000 workers flocked to these midwestern mills, earning one of the highest weekly rates in the industry. What was the rate?
A: $92 per week.

1954

With hoopla, cowboys, and dignitaries, the Union Stock Yard and Transit Company welcomed its billionth animal to be slaughtered on September 6 and voiced enthusiasm about embarking on its second billion. At that time it was capable of handling 120,000 hogs per day and 40,000 cattle, turning out meat at a rate of 10,000 pounds/minute.

Q: The stockyard never even got close to its second billionth slaughter. How many years later did it cease operation, and why?
A: Seventeen years—it ceased operation in 1971. Advances in refrigeration combined with the decline of railroads made a centralized livestock market obsolete.

Q: Chicago had the world's two largest banks under one roof, the First National Bank of Chicago and Continental Illinois Bank and Trust Company. What on earth did the roof have to do with the size of the banks?
A: Because strict Illinois banking laws forbade branch banking, all operations had to be under one roof, leading to such absurdities as the construction of a bridge between two Continental Bank buildings on South LaSalle Street.

1954

Chicago's leading ball and roller bearing firms—Ahlberg Bearing, Aetna Ball and Roller Bearing, and Bearings Manufacturing Company—led the nation by a wide margin in the manufacture of ball and roller bearings.

1955

Ray Kroc, a 52-year-old Chicagoan who had left Oak Park High School without graduating, was out selling Multimixers, a machine capable of mixing five milk shakes simultaneously, when he called on a short-order California restaurant owned by Dick and Mac McDonald. "They had people standing in line, clamoring for more," he later recalled. Kroc franchised their restaurant, finally buying them out in 1961 for $2.7 million and, in turn, grossing $6 million.

Q: What made the customers stand in line at the original McDonald's?
A: The hamburgers cost only 15 cents, half the going price at other restaurants.

Q: Where and when did the first franchised McDonald's open?
A: It opened on April 15 at 400 Lee Street, Des Plaines. It sold hamburgers for $.15 apiece, and it made ten of them to a pound of ground beef. The building is now a museum.

McDonald's is not a restaurant. It's a hamburger business. It's a religion.
RAY KROC

Q: Kroc may never have graduated from high school, but a famous Chicago-born filmmaker with whom he served in the Red Cross during World War I has a Chicago school named after him. Name the school and the filmmaker.
A: The Disney Magnet School on Lake Shore Drive north of Irving Park is named after Walt Disney.

Q: What famous writer from Oak Park also served in the Red Cross during that war?
A: Ernest Hemingway.

1976

Employment in the Chicago area was 2,450,597.

1978

John D. MacArthur died. A notorious penny pincher, he owned 12 major insurance companies, more land than anyone else in Florida, plus untold other banks, airplanes, and plants. At the time of his death he was considered one of America's few billionaires.

Be honest, and work like a son of a bitch.
JOHN D. MACARTHUR

Q: The bulk of MacArthur's estate went to establish the Chicago-based foundation that bears his name. What is the unique difference between it and other foundations?
A: The MacArthur Foundation is the only one that awards some of its grants to people who cannot apply for them—the MacArthur Fellow, or so-called "genius" grants.

1984

On September 6 Walgreen's celebrated the opening of its one-thousandth store. As of 1993 it had some 1,600 stores in twenty-nine states and Puerto Rico and was the nation's largest drugstore chain.

1986

Employment in the Chicago area was 2,654,786, more than the population of the city itself.

1990

Chicago was home to more important medical associations than any other city, including the American Medical Association, the American Hospital Association, the American College of Surgeons, the American College of Radiology, the American Society of Anesthesiologists, the Association of American Physicians & Surgeons, the American Association of Industrial Physicians & Surgeons, and the College of American Pathologists.

Q: Why are so many associations headquartered in Chicago?
A: The central location of Chicago is only part of the story. The whole idea of the professional association was born at the World's Columbian Exposition when the many "congresses" held there led directly to the formation of the first such organizations.

1992

Employment in the Chicago area was 2,982,370, still more than the population of the city.

CHAPTER 3

The Best Game in Town

The mayor is but the right arm of the law, and there should be nothing of human ambition to paralyze the power of that arm.

JOHN WENTWORTH, MAYOR 1857-59

Chicago ain't ready for reform!

ALDERMAN MATHIAS "PADDY" BAULER, UPON HEARING OF
THE DEFEAT OF REFORM MAYOR MARTIN H. KENNELLY
BY RICHARD J. DALEY IN 1955

Good government is good politics.

RICHARD J. DALEY, MAYOR, 1955-76

Chicago is known for its interesting politics and for good reason. What other city can boast such colorful mayors, notorious wheeler-dealer politicos, questionable elections, smoke-filled-room skullduggery, and amazing national party conventions?

Chicago continued to be run by machine politics long after New York's Tammany Hall, the Prendergast machine in Kansas City, the Curley gang in Boston, and a dozen similar organizations had faded away. The legendary machine under Richard J. Daley clung to power and flexed its considerable muscle right up into the 1970s.

Was Chicago as corrupt as its image? Possibly, but as several historians have pointed out, corruption and reform do not always mean the same thing to all people. The great power of the Cook County Democratic machine was always based on its ability to get the goods to its constituents. Whether it was a job or a fixed streetlight, a building permit or a new garbage can on election day, the precinct captain and the alderman made City Hall accessible to the average Joe. Help and understanding were only a telephone call away for the loyal, and what drove so many self-styled reformers crazy was that the people whom they saw as being exploited did not feel exploited. On the contrary, they felt included. As the first Mayor Richard Daley put it, "Good government is good politics."

This observation notwithstanding, the Cook County machine was oiled with money and bribes, and the number of alderman and city officials who have been led to prison over the years is certain testimony to a level of corruption unsurpassed by any other American city. Today, thanks to population shifts, court decisions, and legal reforms, the Chicago machine is dead. Today, Chicago is cleaner than it ever has been—and perhaps just a shade blander as well.

1837

Russell E. Heacock, who cast the only vote against Chicago being incorporated as a town, was the city's first lawyer.

1837

The first election for mayor took place. Recent arrival William B. Ogden, 31, who once served as a New York state senator, defeated John Harris Kinzie, 33, the eldest son of early settler John Kinzie.

> *When you are dealing with Chicago property, the proper way is to go in for all you can get and then go on with your business and forget about it. It will take care of itself.*
> MAYOR WILLIAM B. OGDEN

1837

Ogden is credited with keeping the city solvent during a recession in 1837, introducing the first railroad to Chicago, and later founding both the Chicago Dock and Canal Company and the Chicago and North Western Railroad.

Q: How long did Ogden serve as mayor?
A: Only one year; until 1863 mayors were elected for a one-year term.
Most of Odgen's accomplishments came after his term as mayor.

1840

The Chicago Anti-Slavery Society was formed. Ten years later, the Chicago City Council resolved that its police force would not enforce the Fugitive Slave Law, calling it "a cruel and unjust law [which] ought not be respected by an intelligent community."

1843

John Wentworth, one of the city's first newspaper editors and a giant of a man some six feet six inches tall and weighing 300 pounds, became the first member of Congress elected from Chicago. Only 28 years of age, he was also the youngest man in Congress at the time.

1848

In a border dispute with its northern neighbor, which was seeking statehood at the time, Illinois temporarily lost nine counties to Wisconsin. Cook County and Chicago voted to remain with Illinois, and the other counties decided to stay here, too.

1855

The Beer Hall Riots were triggered by the decision of Mayor Levi Boone, a prominent member of the Know-Nothing Party, to close beer halls on Sundays and raise the price of liquor licenses. A highly conservative mid-nineteenth-century political movement opposed to Catholics and foreigners, the Know-Nothings were influential in creating the Republican Party five years later.

Q: Mayor Boone was a relative of what other famed American westerner?
A: He was the grandnephew of Daniel Boone.

1857

"Long John" was elected mayor. Chicago's tallest mayor, he had an ego to match his size. When asked how he had felt sitting next to the Prince of Wales at a banquet, Wentworth replied, "He sat next to me."

Believing that the best way to repeal an obnoxious law was to enforce it, Wentworth gathered a group of policemen to enforce an ordinance against low-hanging signs and awnings. The group patrolled the city's sidewalks, tearing down every offending sign and awning and telling store owners they could retrieve them if they paid their fines.

Q: What epitaph did Wentworth want on his tomb?
A: None, he said, because nothing there would encourage people to ask whose grave it was. "Being informed that it is John Wentworth's monument, they will ransack old records or visit old libraries to find out who John Wentworth was. When they have found out, they will remember."

1858

The famous Lincoln-Douglas Debates were held at locations across Illinois, but not in Chicago. Later Lincoln did debate Senator Stephen A. Douglas in Chicago, where the latter made his home. Afterward, the *Chicago Tribune* reported that Lincoln had "knocked Douglas higher than a kite," thus helping to establish the *Tribune's* reputation—editor Joseph Medill was a fervid Lincoln supporter—as a newspaper that put politics before facts.

Q: Medill had a stake in these debates. What was it?
A: Medill was one of the founders of the Republican Party, and he urged it to hold its second convention in Chicago and to nominate Lincoln.

1860

Chicago attracted its first political convention, that of the new Republican Party, which of course nominated Abraham Lincoln as president. To host the gathering, a building called the Wigwam was hastily constructed at Lake and Market (now Franklin) Streets. The convention attracted 30,000 people who paid from $1.50 to $2.50 a night for bed and board at city hotels.

Q: How many ballots did it take to nominate Lincoln?
A: Lincoln won the nomination on the third ballot, defeating former New York Governor William Seward, who was the front-running candidate before the convention.

Q: Since 1860 Chicago has been host to more political conventions than any other city. How many has it hosted, and what city is its closest competitor?
A: Chicago has hosted 25 national political conventions (21 for major parties and four for third parties). The city's closest competitor for conventions is Baltimore, which has hosted 10.

Q: The election in 1860 was a four-way race, with two Illinoisans running against each other. Who were the other candidates, and what parties did they represent?
A: In addition to Lincoln, they were Stephen A. Douglas, also from Illinois (Democratic—northern faction), John C. Breckinridge of Kentucky (Democratic—southern faction), and John Bell, from Tennessee (Constitutional Union).

1860

In this historic election Lincoln carried Cook County with 14,589 votes. Douglas received 9,846 in his home county.

1861

While drumming up support for the Union cause, Stephen A. Douglas, known to many as the "Little Giant," died of typhoid fever in the Tremont House in Chicago.

Q: The site of Douglas's home became infamous during the Civil War because the land was put to what purpose? Where was his land located, and what marks the spot now?

A: Camp Douglas was the largest prisoner-of-war camp run by the Union army. It was located near 35th Street and Cottage Grove Avenue and at its peak held some 20,000 Confederate prisoners. Several thousand Confederates died at the camp. A park and statue of Douglas mark the spot today.

Q: A rumored conspiracy to free Confederate prisoners implicated two former Chicago mayors. Who were they, and what was the outcome of the rumor?

A: Because of their Southern sympathies, Buckner Morris, Chicago's second mayor, and Levi Boone were the object of the rumors. It was revealed later that the rumor was a fiction created by Colonel Benjamin Sweet, Camp Douglas's commandant, as a way to further his own career.

1863

Like many other early Chicagoans, William Ogden had switched to the Republican Party because he opposed slavery. Later, Ogden left the party after a disagreement with President Lincoln over the issuance of the Emancipation Proclamation, which Ogden felt was premature.

1865

When the Lincoln Funeral Train arrived in Chicago, 36,000 people viewed the assassinated president's body as it lay in state at the Court House. This was more than twice the number of Cook County voters who had cast ballots for Lincoln in the 1860 election.

Q: The train that carried Lincoln's body included an elegant new sleeping car called the *Pioneer*. It was designed by an industrious Chicagoan. What was his name?

A: He was George Pullman, and the car was a prototype of those the Pullman Palace Car Company would start producing two years later.

1871

In the wake of the Great Chicago Fire, *Tribune* editor Joseph Medill was elected mayor on the Fireproof Ticket.

1973

Medill, associated with the right-wing Law and Order League, ordered saloons and the popular Exposition Hall to be closed on Sundays. This and other unpopular actions made Medill a one-term mayor.

Q: How did these Sunday closing ordinances, which were known as "Blue Laws," figure in the ethnic politics of early Chicago?

A: Some of the New England Protestants, Medill among them, who formed Chicago's first political and commercial elite tended to blame alcohol for poverty or dissipation. The city's major ethnic groups, mainly Irish and Germans who were Lutherans and Catholics, felt that time in a beer garden or a saloon was a perfectly respectable way to spend a Sunday afternoon.

1873

John Jones, regarded as the heartland's wealthiest African-American in the years after the Civil War, was elected a Cook County commissioner. He was the first black person to hold elective office in Cook County and in the state of Illinois.

Q: Jones was buried in a North Side cemetery along with countless other prominent Chicagoans, from Bertha Palmer to Mies van der Rohe. What is its name, and where is it located?

A: It is Graceland Cemetery, at Clark Street and Irving Park Road.

1879

Carter Henry Harrison I began his first of five terms as mayor. Widely admired for his personal honesty, he had a live-and-let-live attitude toward gambling and prostitution, which kept his support high during Chicago's boom years.

Q: What 20th-century mayor, similarly known for personal honesty as well as the ability to ignore corruption all around him, also won election five times?

A: Richard J. Daley.

1886

The Haymarket Riot broke out when police attempted to break up a labor rally on May 4. A bomb—thought to have been the first dynamite bomb ever used in a U.S. protest action—killed several people. Eight men were later convicted of anarchy in a blatantly rigged trial. Four of the defendants—August Spies, Adolph Fischer, George Engel, and Albert R. Parsons—were hanged after the trial.

Q: By the late 19th century, Chicago was a major center for leftist publishing in the English-speaking world. Why?

A: Many radical ideas had their source in Germany, the homeland of a large number of Chicago's laborers. Additionally, Chicago's rapidly growing industries had attracted many laborers who believed that organizing could improve working.

1892

John Peter Altgeld became Illinois's first foreign-born governor and the first from Chicago. A lawyer and real estate developer in the Lakeview neighborhood, he first came to public attention in 1884 with the publication of his booklet called *Our Penal Machinery and Its Victims.* Altgeld believed that incarceration was more likely to turn criminals into repeat offenders than to rehabilitate them. After his term ended he became a law partner of Clarence Darrow, who shared Altgeld's opposition to the death penalty.

Q: For what action during his term in office did the *Chicago Tribune* charge that the German-born Altgeld had "not one drop of pure American blood in his veins"?

A: He pardoned the three remaining Haymarket Riot prisoners, claiming that the police had introduced perjured testimony to convict them.

1893

Mayor Carter Harrison was assassinated by Patrick Prendergast, a disgruntled office seeker, three days before the Columbian Exposition closed. Prendergast was hanged on July 13, 1894.

There are men in this city who pose as reformers who regularly permit the assessors to value their whole property for less than they paid for the pictures on their walls, who cheat the city, then thank God they are not thieves, like the aldermen.

MAYOR CARTER HARRISON, DURING HIS ACRIMONIOUS 1983 MAYORAL CAMPAIGN AGAINST MILLIONAIRE MEATPACKER SAMUEL ALLERTON

1894

When workers struck the Pullman Palace Car Company, the nation's trains (and hence its mail delivery) stopped. Over the strong protest of Governor Altgeld, President Grover Cleveland sent troops from Fort Sheridan to disperse the strikers.

1896

William Jennings Bryan delivered his famous "Cross of Gold" speech at the Democratic National Convention in Chicago. The candidate's speech attracted both laborers and farmers. By touting a gold standard for U.S. currency, a policy that favored the wealthy, Republicans cemented the support of the business class.

1897

Carter Henry Harrison II became the first mayor born in Chicago. He also became the first son to follow in his father's footsteps as Chicago mayor, and eventually he would serve even longer than his father's five terms. Chicago's population had grown to 1,490,937 by the time of his election, and his challenge became one of dealing with growing pains rather than with growth itself, which was his father's chief challenge.

1895

Chicago's First Ward, which included both the Loop and the center of the city's vice district, was ruled by its two alderman, Michael "Hinky Dink" Kenna and "Bathhouse" John Coughlin. Kenna's saloon, at the corner of Clark and Van Buren Streets, was the real seat of power in the First Ward.

Q: What major building is located at that intersection today?
A: Fittingly enough, the Metropolitan Correctional Center stands there, with its triangular shape and slit windows.

Q: What infamous fundraiser were Kenna and Coughlin known for?

A: The First Ward Ball, an annual affair that featured pimps, pickpockets, gamblers, and thieves—and raised around $50,000 in campaign funds each year.

I doubt if any city in the world at any time ever permitted such a disgraceful orgy to be carried on.
ARTHUR BARRAGE FARWELL, PRESIDENT OF THE LAW AND
ORDER LEAGUE, REFERRING TO THE FIRST WARD BALL.

Q: How did Kenna and Coughlin get their nicknames?

A: "Hinky Dink" Michael Kenna got his nickname from his diminutive stature and "Bathhouse" John Coughlin received his from his start working as a "rubber"—the people who rubbed clients dry—in a bathhouse.

Q: Good businessmen that they were, Kenna and Coughlin had fixed scales of tribute for houses of prostitution. What were they?

A: Small houses paid $25 weekly while larger houses handed over $50 to $100 weekly, plus $25 if drinks were sold and another $25 if poker and craps were played. Were the pair asked to stop a grand larceny indictment, the charge was a full $500.

Q: Many of the brothels were "panel houses." Where did the name come from?

A: From a sliding panel built into a wall of the brothel's rooms. Through it, customers pockets were picked while they were being "entertained" in the room.

A Republican is a man who wants you to go to church every Sunday.

A Democrat says if a man wants a glass of beer, he can have it....

I ain't going to be unethicult for nobody.

"BATHHOUSE" JOHN COUGHLIN

1906

Marshall Field died, leaving an estate valued at $120 million, which was by far the largest of the fortunes piled up by Chicago's 19th-century moguls.

Q: How did other Chicago estates compare?

A: The Cyrus McCormick (died 1884) fortune amounted to $10 million; Philip Danforth Armour (died 1901) left $31 million; George Mortimer Pullman (died 1897) left $21 million.

1915

William Hale "Big Bill" Thompson won his first term as mayor of Chicago, was reelected in 1919, and after sitting out a term in 1923, was reelected again in 1927. Often dismissed as a buffoon, Thompson also presided over a program of urban beautification, as many plaques on Michigan Avenue and Wacker Drive testify.

Q: Thompson was also called "the man who plays with sailboats." Why?

A: Three years running, from 1908 to 1910, Thompson won the Mackinaw

Race. In the last year he set a record of 31.5 hours, which stood for over 70 years.

Q: What did Thompson do after his defeat in 1931?
A: He ran one more time in 1939, but his reputation as a corruptible rogue had undermined his popularity.

1919

The Communist Party of the United States was founded in Chicago.

1920

At 2:00 A.M. on the morning of June 11, Republican Party leaders meeting in Suite 404-5-6 of the Blackstone Hotel chose Warren G. Harding as the party's nominee.

Q: How did this suite enter American political lore?
A: The considerable number of cigars consumed during the secret deliberations led to a new political term—the "smoke-filled room."

1923

William E. Dever, a widely respected judge and former alderman, was elected mayor as a Democrat pledging to reform the corruption at that time associated with the Republican Party. One of his principal supporters was Clarence Darrow, who told Dever "Chicago needs a mayor who has the courage to say 'no' and say it to all his friends." Upon the election of Dever, Al Capone and his associates promptly moved their headquarters out of the city to Cicero.

1923

The Chicago City Council voted to secede from Illinois as a protest against a proposed new state constitution. The ploy flopped, but so did the constitution, by a 5-1 margin of the popular vote.

1927

Dever struggled to control bootlegging, but to no avail. "Big Bill" Thompson defeated him in his bid for reelection by promising not only to reopen the speakeasies that Dever had closed, but to open "10,000 new ones." One of Thompson's strongest supporters was Al Capone.

They was trying to beat Bill with the better element vote. The trouble with Chicago is that there ain't much better element.
    WILL ROGERS, ECHOING THE NATION'S SURPRISE AT DEVER'S DEFEAT

Q: Thompson's supporters celebrated the triumph of the "wet" vote in a most appropriate fashion on election night. Where?

A: They gathered at the Fish Fans Club, a floating speakeasy in Belmont Harbor, which became so overloaded with revelers that it sank. No one drowned. Al Capone did not attend.

1928

Oscar DePriest, an Alabama-born Chicagoan, became the first black from a northern state to serve in Congress. He had also been the first African-American to serve on the Chicago City Council and on the Cook County Board of Commissioners.

1931

Anton J. Cermak became Chicago's first and only foreign-born mayor by defeating Thompson, 671,189 to 476,922. Cermak's staunch stand against blue laws led the *Chicago Tribune* to call him "the wettest man in Chicago."

> *I am glad it was me instead of you.*
> CERMAK'S WORDS AFTER HE WAS HIT BY AN ASSASSIN'S
> BULLET USUALLY THOUGHT TO HAVE BEEN INTENDED
> FOR PRESIDENT-ELECT FRANKLIN D. ROOSEVELT

Q: Cermak's assassination remains the subject of conflicting opinion. What was the name of the assassin, who might his real target have been, and how did Cermak die?

A: Cermak's opposition to the mob's grip on Chicago has led some to speculate that he, not Roosevelt, was assassin Giuseppe Zangara's real target. Cermak didn't die for 21 days, and there was some speculation that his death was caused as much by a preexisting ulcerative colitis as it was by the bullet.

Q: What happened to the assassin?

A: Zangara was tried and convicted in less than 40 days, and he was executed just two weeks after Cermak died.

Q: What was Cermak's greatest political accomplishment?

A: He united the city's ethnic and Catholic voting blocs with the black vote to create the Democratic machine that ruled Chicago for 50 years.

1933

President Franklin Delano Roosevelt called the West Side 24th Ward "the best Democratic ward in the country."

Q: Who was responsible for Democratic solidarity of the 24th Ward?

A: It was Jacob Arvey, the son of a Maxwell Street peddler who used the ward as a home base during his rise to statewide political prominence. Avery also founded the once prominent law firm of Arvey and Hodes.

Put people under obligation to you. Make them your friends.

JACOB ARVEY

1932

Henry Horner was elected Illinois's first, and to date only, Jewish governor.

Q: A housing project named for Henry Horner figured in a book published a few years ago that was turned into a TV movie starring a talk show hostess whose studio is located about halfway between the project and Lake Michigan. Name the book, its author, and the star.

A: *There Are No Children Here,* Alex Kotlowitz, and Oprah Winfrey.

He was the real goods. In the realm of politics there have been too few like him. He collaborated with men who were purchasable without becoming purchasable himself. He had thorough-going integrity. He got to high places without selling his soul.

CARL SANDBURG, EULOGIZING HENRY HORNER IN 1940

Q: What hobby did Sandburg and Horner share?

A: They collected items pertaining to Abraham Lincoln. Horner left his materials to the state of Illinois. Today, the Illinois State Library's Lincoln collection is second only to that of the Library of Congress.

1935

Edward J. Kelly, appointed to fill out Cermak's term, was elected mayor in his own right on April 1. During his 14 years in office, he cemented the hold of Cermak's ethnic machine and enlisted the support of many businessmen, including the arch-conservative publisher of the *Chicago Tribune,* Robert McCormick.

Q: Prior to becoming mayor, Edward J. Kelly had served as president of the South Park Board. Which of the following were accomplished during his tenure there?

1. The beautification of Grant Park, including the construction of Buckingham Fountain.
2. The construction of the Shedd Aquarium.

3. The construction of the Adler Planetarium.
4. The opening of the Garfield Park Conservatory.
5. The construction of Soldier Field.
6. The renovation of the Museum of Science and Industry.

A: All but number 4. At the time, Chicago had three park boards. As a Bridgeport native, Kelly was a member of the South Park Board; Garfield Park fell under the jurisdiction of the West Park Board.

Q: Mayor Edward J. Kelly had a heart attack and died while on a routine visit to his doctor three years after leaving office. What other mid-century mayor died in similar circumstances, but while still in office?
A: Richard J. Daley.

The time is not far away when we shall forget the color of a man's skin and see him only in the light of intelligence of his mind and soul.
MAYOR EDWARD J. KELLY, 1946

1936

Richard J. Daley won his first election, a write-in campaign, for state representative.

Q: On which ticket did Daley run?
A: The Republican ticket. The formal candidate had died during the campaign, so Daley staged a successful write-in effort. He switched back to the Democratic Party as soon as he had assumed office.

1937

Mathias "Paddy" Bauler was elected city collector. When he was caught collecting license fees from ineligible businesses and neglecting to issue the licenses as well, Bauler replied "What the hell! I ain't doing nothing that every politician in this town ain't done for a hundred years. And I ain't apologizing for it, neither."

Q: Paddy Bauler's political headquarters was in a saloon. Where was it located?
A: At the corner of North Avenue and Sedgwick, in the German neighborhood. Today that area is part of Old Town.

Q: Bauler was no fan of reformers. What did he call them?
A: "Political science kids."

Q: A popular Old Town folksinger wrote a classic song about Bauler and his brand of politics. Who was he, and what is the song?

A: Win Stracke, one of the founders of the Old Town School of Folk Music, wrote "The Forty-Third Ward."

1946

Richard J. Daley lost his only election, a bid to become Cook County Sheriff.

1947

Jacob Avery and other political bosses dumped Kelly in favor of another Bridgeportian, Martin H. Kennelly, to run for mayor as a "reformer." To their surprise, Kennelly was indeed a reformer, and they regretted their choice immediately.

1955

With the backing of the machine, Richard J. Daley defeated Kennelly in the mayoral primary. He won the general election and went on to serve as mayor longer than anyone else in Chicago history—21 years in all.

You can't give that guy a nickel, that's how honest he is.
STATE SENATOR WILLIAM "BOTCHY" CONNORS, SPEAKING OF DALEY

Q: Daley remained mayor so long, he acquired more than his share of nicknames. Name some.

A: Boss, Da Mare, Hizzoner, The Man on Five, the Great Dumpling.

Q: Mayor Daley's license plate became famous. What was it?

A: Until his death in 1976, Daley rode in a car with plate number 708 220, the number of votes he received in his first campaign for mayor.

Q: Although Chicago's aldermen have come from all fields of endeavor, only one was an Olympic gold medalist. Who was he?

A: Ralph Metcalfe shared a gold medal with Jessie Owens in the 1936 Olympics, and he won an aldermanic seat in 1955. When Metcalfe later asserted his independence, Mayor Daley refused to support him, but the alderman was reelected anyway.

Ladies and Gentlemen of the League of Women Voters.
MAYOR RICHARD J. DALEY

Gentlemen, remember, the policeman isn't there to create disorder. He is there to preserve disorder.

RICHARD J. DALEY'S INFAMOUS MISSTATEMENT DURING
THE 1968 DEMOCRATIC NATIONAL CONVENTION

They should have printed what he meant, not what he said.

EARL BUSH, DALEY'S SPOKESMAN, CONCERNING THE NEWS MEDIA REPORTING
ON THE MAYOR'S "SHOOT TO KILL" ORDER DURING THE 1968 RIOTS ON THE
WEST SIDE THAT FOLLOWED MARTIN LUTHER KING'S ASSASSINATION

1956

Mayor Richard J. Daley nominated John F. Kennedy for vice president at the Democratic convention held in Chicago.

Q: What Illinoisan ended up on the Democratic ticket that year?
A: Former Governor Adlai E. Stevenson ran for president. As in 1952, he lost to Dwight D. Eisenhower.

1960

John F. Kennedy beat Richard M. Nixon in Illinois, 2,377,846 to 2,368,988 amid charges that Mayor Daley had engineered vote fraud in Cook County to elect his fellow Irish-American. The charges were never proven, but they are widely accepted as truth.

1969

Lilian Piatrowski was elected the first female committeeman in the history of the Democratic Central Committee of Cook County.

1976

Richard J. Daley suffered a heart attack in his doctor's office and died shortly thereafter. The city council chose Alderman Michael Bilandic, the mild-mannered man from Daley's old 11th Ward, to replace him.

1979

Michael Bilandic was defeated in the Democratic primary by Jane M. Byrne, a city hall worker who had never before run for elective office.

Q: What issue did Byrne exploit to achieve her upset victory?
A: The ineptitude of city crews in clearing the streets after a record 50 inches of snowfall.

1983

In the highest voter turnout in Chicago history—88 percent—Mayor Byrne lost the Democratic mayoral primary to U.S. Representative Harold Washington, a member of Congress from Illinois's First District. Richard J. Daley's son, Richard, also lost in the same contest. Washington became the city's first African-American mayor.

Q: What was the connection between Daley's death and Washington's victory?
A: Bilandic had edged out Wilson Frost, a popular black alderman and president pro tem of the council, in the rush to succeed Daley. Black leaders remembered this slight, and they built a Reform coalition around Washington.

Q: Washington's contentious first term earned a famous nickname. What was it, and who coined it?
A: Comedian Aaron Freeman came up with the term *council wars* after the movie *Star Wars.*

1985

Vito Marzullo, alderman of the 25th Ward on the South Side, retired after serving for 32 years (1953-85). He is credited with first using the term *foot soldiers* for the army of precinct captains who were his links to his ward, and for his pithy observations. For instance, "Those who know the least speak the most" and "Do good and forget, do bad and remember."

The intellectuals, the millionaires, the obstructionists, they messed it up. They redrew my ward and they used cats and dogs and mouses and counted them as people.
VITO MARZULLO, UPON RETIRING AS 25TH WARD ALDERMAN IN 1985

He says he don't want no machine.
MARZULLO'S DISDAINFUL REFERENCE TO MAYOR
WASHINGTON'S 1983 REFORM AGENDA

1987

In November Mayor Harold Washington died of a heart attack, and the city council once again had to elect a successor. It chose Eugene Sawyer, a black alderman, who served until 1989.

Q: Where did Washington die?

A: After collapsing in his office, he was rushed to Northwestern Memorial Hospital, where he was treated by the same cardiovascular surgeon who had treated Richard Daley nearly nine years earlier.

1989

The *Chicago Tribune,* which in 1948 had printed the erroneous headline "Dewey Defeats Truman," made another blooper when it reported that the 91-year-old Marzullo had died. It was reported that Marzullo's only response to reading the story was that it had ruined his breakfast. Marzullo died on his own schedule in 1990.

1989

After a year and a half of Eugene Sawyer's leadership, Richard M. Daley ran in a special election held to fill the rest of Washington's term. He won against two opponents and was reelected in 1991 and 1995.

Q: Another father and son combination ran for mayor but lost, each time to part of another mayoral father and son pair. Name the pair, their opponents, and the most noticeable—if superficial—difference between them and the winners.

A: University of Chicago professor and alderman Charles E. Merriam was defeated by Carter Harrison II in 1911. His son, Robert E. Merriam, was defeated by Richard J. Daley in 1955. Conicidentally, the winning mayors had the same names (Carter Harrison and Richard Daley) as the other half of their family mayoral duos, while the losing ones (Charles and Robert) didn't.

CHAPTER 4

No Sissy Town

The young city is not only vigorous, but she laves her beautiful limbs daily in Lake Michigan and comes out clean and pure every morning.

MAYOR CARTER HENRY HARRISON I

This here's a frontier town. The church and the WCTU never growed no big town yet.

GEORGE WELLINGTON STREETER, RAPSCALLION
RULER OF HIS OWN VICE DISTRICT

Chicago ain't no sissy town!

ALDERMAN MICHAEL "HINKY DINK" KENNA

No other part of Chicago's history is as famous as its crime. To this day, people around the world still make a "rat-a-tat-tat" machine-gun noise when they hear mention of the Windy City. The reputation certainly is based in truth—from the Gilded Age through the Roaring Twenties, Chicago led America in the number of its brothels, speakeasies, and gangland slayings. The reason? Chicago led America in everything else, and it was only natural that it should have led in crime as well.

That Chicago has been stuck with its gangster image is due to another fact—its lawless period coincided with the world's first great media boom. When the last of the 1920s bootleggers had long since gone to his (no doubt, much deserved) reward, movies such as *Scarface* and *Public Enemy Number One* were still running on the late show. The tommy gun and the gin mill entered American mythology right alongside the cowboy and the covered wagon. Gangsters are no more representative of Chicago today than sod houses are of Nebraska, but both images are hard to shake.

1674

Among Chicago's first French nonnative visitors was a fur trapper named Pierre Moreau, who is recalled today as Chicago's first bootlegger. Reportedly an agent for the governor of New France, one of whose ventures was selling liquor illegally to the Native Americans, Moreau was sent to expand the governor's operations into Illinois.

Q: What is the origin of the word *bootlegger?*
A: In the 17th century, smugglers of contraband liquor often carried it in the upper part of their high boots.

1833

One of Chicago's first actions after it organized itself as a town was to build a jail, which was made of logs. In November of that first year an ordinance was passed to fine owners $2 any time their hogs, pigs, or sows ran at large through the town.

1834

In the young city's first murder trial, an Irishman, according to contemporary reports, was acquitted on a charge of killing his wife.

1834

Chicago enacted its first blue law: a $5 fine for keeping a tippling house or grocery open on Sunday.

1840

John Stone, the first murderer to be convicted in Cook County, was hanged June 10 on the open prairie three miles south of town. The public hanging reportedly drew a large crowd.

Q: What stands on the site of the hanging today?
A: It is likely the hanging took place just north of Michael Reese Hospital, where the Prairie Shores apartment complex is located.

1847

The city jail, described as "a number of woodsheds and corn cribs most cozily clustered in a huge whitewashed pound" by a contemporary source, was apparently no more effective than aesthetically pleasing. Three prisoners were reported to have escaped by burrowing out through the floor.

1848

The first U.S. court opened, presided over by Judge Nathaniel Pope. One year earlier, the city's first law school had opened.

1853

Allan Pinkerton, who had established his National Detective Agency in 1850, reported that he was the object of an assassination attempt on September 5. Self-righteous and a self-promoter to boot, he is said to have claimed the "authority of the Eternal" when he arrested a pickpocket in 1857. The man was later convicted.

Q: Pinkerton settled soon after his 1842 arrival from Scotland in a far northwestern suburb named after a city in Scotland. Name the town.
A: It was Dundee, now the home of Santa's Village Amusement Park.

Q: What was the original purpose of Pinkerton's detective agency?
A: An ardent abolitionist, he established the agency to aid runaway slaves.

1854

Roger Plant ran Chicago's first underworld gambling and prostitution mob from a club called Under the Willow at Wells and Monroe Streets.

Q: What was the motto that Plant had emblazoned on his window shades?
A: "Why Not?"

1855

Religion, ethnic differences, and the thirst for alcohol led to one of Chicago's most colorful incidents, the Beer Hall Riots. On March 17 Mayor Levi Boone, a Protestant and temperance advocate, declared that Sunday closing laws for taverns would be enforced. In addition he raised the price of liquor licenses from $50 to $300. The city's German saloon owners, for the most part Catholics, were arrested for refusing to obey. In support several hundred Germans marched on city hall, but Mayor Boone was ready for them. As the demonstrators crossed the Clark Street Bridge Boone ordered the bridge opened, splitting the marchers in half. In the clash with police that followed one man was killed and several were wounded. All told, 70 rioters were arrested, a dozen tried, and on June 15 most were acquitted. Teetotaling Protestants would clash with Chicago's Catholic ethnics over temperance many times in future years until the Irish took firm command of city hall and the issue evaporated.

Q: Closing saloons is not how Chicagoans observe March 17 today. What is?

A: The last thing Chicagoans would consider doing on St. Patrick's Day is close saloons. Instead, they dye the Chicago River green.

1857

On April 20 Mayor Wentworth, aggravated by low-hanging awnings and signs on commercial buildings, decided to enforce a city regulation against them. The legend goes that Wentworth ordered police to gather them up in a nocturnal roundup. Storekeepers who paid fines were allowed to claim their property.

Q: Why might Wentworth have been particularly offended by the street awnings?

A: Even with his 14-inch boots off, Wentworth stood six feet six inches tall.

1857

In the same year Wentworth, tired of dog fights and sex shows in a red light district known as the Sands, personally lead 30 policemen and hundreds of citizens on a cleanup crusade. Just prior to the raid, Wentworth cunningly arranged for a dog fight to be a advertised in a nearby neighborhood to entice the tougher occupants of the Sands away temporarily. The raiders then demolished every disreputable house.

Q: Where were the Sands, and who owns the land now?

A: The Sands was located north of the river along the lakeshore, on property owned by William Ogden, Chicago's first mayor and a friend of Wentworth's. Thus, the raid was likely an early example of mayoral and real estate interests working together. The land is owned today by the Chicago Dock and Canal Trust, a firm founded by Ogden.

1857

Temperance was a popular cause in early Chicago and teetotaling officials succeeded in raising the cost of liquor licenses from $50 to $100. They had apparently learned their lesson from the Beer Hall Riots and dared not stretch it any higher. The Chicago Temperance Society, an early voluntary association, was formed to encourage total abstinence.

That same year, one John Hohn was fined for violating the provision in Northwestern University's charter that prohibited the sale of distilled spirits anywhere within four miles of its Evanston campus.

Q: One of the oldest buildings on Northwestern's campus was named after the founding president of the Evanston Ladies College, which later became part of the university. She was better known for her affiliation with a group opposed to distilled spirits of any kind. What is her name and the name of the organization?

A: Willard Hall, now the Music School at Northwestern, was named after Frances Willard, who was for 20 years president of the Women's Christian Temperance Union.

1857

A William Jackson was executed for murder on June 19 in the Bull's Head Cattle Yard on Ashland Avenue, one of the city's first meatpacking areas. By then a city of 85,000, Chicago had a police force of 92 men, distributed so that each of the city's divisions had a captain, three lieutenants, three second lieutenants, four bell ringers, and a fire policeman.

A major fire at the Holt and Mason lumberyard on Market Street in January was discovered to have been set by a fireman known as "Beast" Brown. The lumberyard owners apparently had not subscribed to the firemen's ball, sponsored by Brown's engine company. The incendiary fireman later went to the penitentiary, but not before implicating two other men.

On July 1 one Michael McNamee was hanged in the courthouse for murdering his wife. His was Chicago's first nonpublic execution.

Q: Where was the courthouse located?

A: The same place it is today, between Clark, Lake, Randolph, and LaSalle Streets. The walls of the courthouse, erected in 1853, were one of the few structures left standing after the Great Fire in 1871.

1861

Claiming to have heard rumors of an assassination attempt, Allan Pinkerton spirited Abraham Lincoln into Washington on the eve of his inauguration. A grateful President Lincoln later asked Pinkerton to head the U.S. Secret Service.

Q: In the 1870s, Pinkerton turned to writing fiction that dramatized his detectives' work. One of his stories set among Irish miners in Pennsylvania became a movie starring Sean Connery and Richard Harris in 1969. Name it.

A: *The Molly McGuires.*

Q: Pinkerton's motto—"The Eye That Never Sleeps"—led to a popular name for detectives still used today. What is it?

A: Private eye.

Q: Pinkerton is said to have fled Scotland to avoid incarceration for radical activities, but a Pinkerton man eventually represented something rather different to common laborers struggling to get a better deal from their employers. What was it?

A: Pinkerton men were hired by employers to break up union organizing.

1864

The Union army built a prisoner-of-war camp named after Stephen A. Douglas, the fiery senator who had left his South Side estate to the federal government upon his death in 1861. Chicagoans concerned about Confederate prisoners' plight donated food and clothing to them regularly. In 1864 a Confederate master spy named Thomas Hines hatched a plot to spring many of the prisoners and disrupt President Lincoln's 1864 reelection. The plot fizzled, but the *Chicago Tribune* used it to sell quite a few newspapers.

1879

Kentucky-born and Yale-educated Carter Henry Harrison I was elected mayor, the first non-New Englander to hold the job. Feeling that vice was inevitable, he worked to confine it to one area of the city. In this he was quite successful.

You can't make people moral by ordinance and it's no use trying. This is a free town.

MAYOR CARTER HARRISON I

Q: Carter confined most of the city's bordellos and gambling dens to a near-South Side district known as the Levee. How did it get its name?

A: Itinerant gamblers imported the term from the Mississippi River delta country where they had previously plied their trade.

1890

Mickey Finn, a Chicago bartender, invented the infamous drink that would ever after bear his name.

Q: What's in a Mickey Finn and what was it first used for?

A: Finn combined chloral hydrate and snuff water to drug and then rob his clientele.

1892

The World's Columbian Exposition opened on May 1. Determined to avoid lawlessness, the management hired a private police force of 1,700 uniformed officers and 250 undercover agents. In addition they persuaded "King Michael"

McDonald, leader of the city's pickpockets and second-story artists, to have his men ply their trade elsewhere.

Q: How did McDonald enforce his rule over the city's sticky-fingered set?
A: Operating from a four-story gambling/rooming house called the Store, McDonald collected as much as 25 percent of the gambling dens' profits for "protection."

Q: McDonald is credited with creating three famous expressions about separating victims from their money. What were they?
A: "There's a sucker born every minute," "Never give a sucker an even break," and "You can't cheat an honest man."

Q: How did McDonald die?
A: Of a broken heart, when his second wife, Dora—a burlesque dancer 20 years his junior—shot her lover to death on February 21, 1907. McDonald took to bed and lingered until that August, leaving the great bulk of his estate to charity.

1893

May Churchill Sharpe, known as Chicago May and called the world's cleverest crook by police, was an accomplished pickpocket as well as the country's first professional shoplifter. She relieved many a world's fairgoer of jewelry and other valuables, which she concealed in pockets sewn inside her voluminous skirts. She later moved on to New York, London, and Paris where she became the first hussy to have recorded her sexual liaisons on film for use in blackmail schemes.

> *During construction of the fair, we nicked the builders. When the fair opened, we nicked the customers.*
> CHICAGO MAY

> *Oh, woman, woman! You have much to answer for.... Ah, if I had never known Chicago May.*
> A THWARTED LOVER AND FELLOW THIEF WHO LANDED
> IN JAIL WHILE CHICAGO MAY WENT FREE

1894

Vina Fields was a Negro madam who ran the Fields House, the largest brothel in Chicago history. It specialized in "ladies of color." Fields ran the brothel like a settlement house, sharing a greater portion of the proceeds with its "girls" than any similar establishment. In his famous tract *If Christ Came to Chicago,* William Stead cited Fields for her civic pride and devotion to alleviating poverty.

> *Every day this whole winter [1893-94], she has fed a hungry, ragged regiment of out-of-works. The day before I called, 201 men had free dinners of her providing.*
>
> WILLIAM STEAD

Q: Vina Fields was not the only madam known for her good works. Name another.

A: Carrie Watson, who ran one of Chicago's classiest brothels at 441 South Clark Street, is remembered for feeding the destitute during the panic of 1893.

1900

On February 1 the Everleigh Club, which was to be known for the next 12 years as the most elegant bordello in the country, opened in a 50-room mansion at 2131-33 South Dearborn. Its proprietors, two Kentucky-born sisters named Ada and Minna, spent $200,000 refurbishing the mansion. An evening at the Everleigh Club was no casual event. A recommendation was required for admittance, champagne cost $12 a bottle, and any customer who did not spend at least $50 was asked not to return.

> *Be polite, patient, and forget what you are here for. Remember the Everleigh Club has no time for the rough element, the clerk on a holiday, or a man without a checkbook. Your youth and beauty are all you have. Preserve it. Stay respectable at all times.*
>
> FROM THE EVERLEIGH SISTERS'S EMPLOYEE "HANDBOOK"

Q: What was the first night's "take" at the Everleigh Club?
A: $1,000.

> *That's educating the wrong end of a whore.*
>
> BARBED-WIRE MAGNATE JOHN GATES UPON HEARING THAT
THE EVERLEIGH SISTERS' BORDELLO HAD A LIBRARY

> *If it weren't for married men, we couldn't have carried on at all, and if it weren't for cheating married women, we could have made another million.*
>
> THE EVERLEIGH SISTERS

1900

The House of All Nations, a brothel just up the street from the Everleigh Club, had two entrances, one for $5 patrons and one for $2 patrons.

Q: How did the House of All Nations get its name?

A: Many brothels in the Levee went in for ethnic specialization, for instance, black, Japanese, etc. The House of All Nations, however, offered a wide range of ethnic diversity, thus becoming the first politically correct brothel in Chicago history.

The bright lights and seductive allurements beckon the callow youth, and the careless maiden to a swift and certain Death, and in anguish they lift their guilty voices and cry out "Damned! Damned! Damned!"
SAMUEL PAYNTER WILSON, *CHICAGO BY GASLIGHT*

1904

A gambling ship was established on Lake Michigan, the first of its kind in American history. A partner in the venture was "Big Jim" O'Leary, the son of the woman whose cow purportedly started the Chicago Fire. He also succeeded Michael McDonald as king of the Chicago gambling world.

1906

Johann Hoch, known as the Stockyard Bluebeard, was hanged. He had married 24 women between 1892 and 1905 and poisoned half of them after they had signed over their savings to him.

1907

Joseph Weil, a con artist with the unexplained nickname of Yellow Kid, ran his first scam by telephone. One of the schemes he ran shortly after the First World War has been credited as being the first so-called "setup." Weil died unapologetically in Chicago at the age of 100 in 1976.

I never found a man I couldn't take, and any con man knows you can't cheat an honest man. If you expect something for nothing, you'll always wind up on your ass!
JOSEPH "YELLOW KID" WEIL

1909

The last of the infamous First Ward Balls was held. For 11 years aldermen "Hinky Dink" Kenna and "Bathhouse" John Coughlin had sponsored the underworld bacchanal, enriching themselves by up to $50,000 each year.

If a great disaster had befallen the Coliseum last night, there would not have been a second-story worker, a dip or plug-ugly, porch climber, dope fiend, or scarlet woman remaining in Chicago.
A *TRIBUNE* REPORTER COVERING THE BALL IN 1907

1911

In this year, according to a report prepared for Mayor Frank Busse entitled *The Social Evil in Chicago,* there were 282 brothels known to the police and 3,233 known prostitutes. The average age of a prostitute was 20.4 years and her average weekly wage $6. All told, the brothels produced a total annual profit of $15,699,449.

Q: What is Mayor Busse known for today?
A: A highway in Park Ridge, a forest preserve, and a police barge.

The white slave dealers flaunt their dastardly vice in the face of the public, and houses of ill-fame are conducted with a boldness unequaled anywhere in the world.

SAMUEL PAYNTER WILSON

1918

City officials finally managed to evict Captain George Wellington Streeter from the area of gambling and vice dens he had established on a lakefront sandbar at Chicago Avenue. Real estate interests had long coveted the land for expensive development.

Q: What is the area called today?
A: Streeterville.

1919

The worst race riot in Chicago history started July 27 at a South Side beach when a black youth swam into "white" waters. Before it ended four days later, 38 people had been killed and 537 wounded.

1920

On June 21 Carl Wanderer shot a supposed thief who was robbing him and his wife. Later, it turned out the man was an actor Wanderer had hired. In love with a 16-year-old girl, he'd expropriated his wife's savings account, and the theft was an apparent ruse to cover her murder. On October 10 of the following year Wanderer went to the gallows for his crimes.

1920

The Volstead Act became law on January 16, and the first official shot in the Chicago bootleg wars was fired on May 11. "Big" Jim Colosimo, an immigrant who had turned a fortuitous marriage to one of the city's leading madams into control over 200 brothels, was shot and killed in his restaurant at

2126 South Wabash Avenue. Johnny Torrio, Colosimo's former associate and the padrone of Al Capone, was suspected because Colosimo had not been paying enough attention to the growing demand for illegal whiskey. Mourners at his funeral included three judges, an assistant state's attorney, and a number of aldermen—as well as Johnny Torrio.

Q: Colosimo's restaurant, popular and classy in its day, introduced what kind of music to Chicago?
A: Jazz, then called jass.

Q: Family connections counted in Chicago. What was the name of Colosimo's wife, and how was she related to his killer?
A: Colosimo had brought Johnny Torrio, a cousin of his wife, Victoria Moresco, to Chicago from New York to handle unpleasant tasks. When Colosimo fell for a pretty, young singer and divorced Victoria, Torrio was enraged. Frankie Yale, a New York associate of Torrio's, is generally credited with "taking out" Colosimo that May evening.

Q: Who was supposedly making a delivery of illegal whiskey to Colosimo when the gang boss was killed?
A: Big "Jim" O'Leary, the son of the lady with the cow, lantern, and barn that were said to have started the Great Chicago Fire in 1871.

1921

Per barrel, bootleg beer cost $5 and sold for $55. Thirsty Chicagoans consumed 20,000 barrels a week, generating millions in profits for gangsters who were prepared to kill in order to protect their lucrative franchises. In the 14 years of Prohibition 703 bootleggers were murdered in the Chicago gangland wars. The first was Colosimo. The second was Steve Wisniewski, who in July was "taken for a one-way ride" to Libertyville, adding a new phrase to the English language.

1921

"Terrible" Tommy O'Connor escaped from Cook County Jail on December 11, the night before he was to be hanged. He was never seen again. He had killed four men (including a Chicago policeman) and inspired a nationwide manhunt before he was arrested. Because he was sentenced to death by hanging, Cook County officials kept the gallows in storage long after the state of Illinois instituted electrocution. In 1977, on the theory that "Terrible" Tommy was a permanent no-show, the gallows was finally given to Donley's Wild West Town in Union, Illinois, where it stands today.

1923

The South Side Saltis-McErlane gang is credited with being the first underworld organization to use the Thompson submachine gun to conduct business.

Q: What is the origin of the tommy gun?
A: It was invented during World War I by a General Thompson, who was appalled at its subsequent use by criminals.

Q: Why was it so popular among gangsters?
A: It was hand-held and highly portable, and its rapid fire eliminated the need for expert marksmanship.

1923

Revenge knows no boundaries. After gangster Samuel "Nails" Morton was killed by a kicking horse on May 13, three of his enraged henchmen led the guilty horse to the spot in Lincoln Park where the accident had occurred and gunned it down.

Q: Who was Nails Morton?
A: A member of Dion O'Banion's North Side bootleg operation and a Maxwell Street native, he had won a Croix de Guerre during World War I.

1924

In May police raided the Sieben Brewery in the 1400 block on North Larrabee. They confiscated 130,000 gallons of illegal brew and arrested 31 bootleggers, including Johnny Torrio and Dion O'Banion. Chicago was awash in beer, much of it made right there in the city. For instance, in Little Hell the district between Sedgwick and the river from Chicago Avenue to Division, hundreds of Italian families made home beer which they sold to Johnny Torrio's mob for 50 cents a gallon.

1924

Mike Merlo, head of Chicago's Unione Siciliana, died on November 8. Schofield's florist shop, on State Street across from Holy Name Cathedral, got several orders for elaborate floral tributes. They included the following: Johnny Torrio $10,000, Al Capone $8,000, Frankie Uale $2,000, and Angelo Genna $750. Uale was head of Brooklyn's Unione Siciliana and Genna was in charge of Little Hell's breweries. On the following Friday 20,000 people, including a mile-long cortege of cars, accompanied Merlo's body to Mt. Carmel Cemetery in Hillside. Honorary pallbearers included the reform mayor, the state's attorney, and Chicago's chief of police.

1924

On November 10 Dion O'Banion was shot in his flower shop opposite Holy Name Cathedral. Three men entered the shop, shots were fired, and O'Banion was killed. Frankie Yale (Uale) was one of the gunmen. On the day after Merlo's burial, O'Banion was sent to rest with an equally lavish display: 20,000 people, 26 trucks full of flowers, and a two-mile-long cortege (more Irish than Italians owned cars, some said). He, too, was buried at Mt. Carmel.

Q: Holy Name Cathedral figured in another gangland incident. Where is it, and what else happened there?

A: Two years later Hymie Weiss (born Earl Wojciechowski), who took over the North Side bootlegging operation after O'Banion's death, was shot while returning to his office above the floral shop. Some of the shots hit the cathedral's front steps.

Q: What was O'Banion's original business?

A: Newspaper circulation. He first worked for the *Tribune,* then switched to the *Herald* and *Examiner,* where he worked for the father of *TV Guide* magnate Walter Annenberg.

1924

Richard A. Loeb and Nathan F. Leopold murdered 14-year old Bobby Franks in an attempt to commit the "perfect" crime.

Q: Leopold and Loeb's connection to the crime was quickly discovered. How?

A: By tracing a pair of eyeglasses found next to Franks's body to the shop that had made them up for Loeb.

Q: The lawyer who defended Leopold and Loeb was involved the following year in Tennessee's famous "monkey" trial. What was his name, and why had he agreed to take the case?

A: They were defended by Clarence Darrow, an ardent foe of capital punishment. His brilliant defense saved the two men from the gallows, a defense made famous in the book and movie *Compulsion.*

Q: What happened to Leopold and Loeb?

A: Loeb died in prison in 1936 during a sexual attack and Leopold was paroled in 1958, when he moved to Puerto Rico and worked in a Church of the Brethren hospital until his death in 1971.

All I want is to find some quiet place where I can sink from sight and live quietly, and serve others to atone for my crime.

NATHAN F. LEOPOLD

1926

Earl "Little Hymie" Weiss, reportedly the only man Al Capone feared, was gunned down on the steps of Holy Name Cathedral.

Q: Who killed Weiss, and why?
A: Weiss had taken over the North Side operation after O'Banion's death and tried to kill Johnny Torrio in revenge, but Torrio and Capone's South Side men got to Weiss first.

1929

The St. Valentine's Day Massacre killed seven members of Bugs Moran's North Side gang in a garage at 2122 North Clark Street. On hearing of the crime, Moran is reported to have said, "Only Capone kills like that."

Q: Who was Bugs Moran, and why was Capone after him?
A: Moran had inherited the North Side operation from Weiss, and Capone wanted to eliminate all competition.

1930

The *Chicago Tribune*'s ace crime reporter, Jake Lingle, was gunned down in the Illinois Central Station entrance at Randolph and Michigan. After his death a large bundle of cash was found in his rooms, and his close ties to Al Capone and other gangland figures became known—much to his employer's embarrassment.

1931

When a 72-year-old black woman was evicted from her home at 5016 South Dearborn, 2,000 blacks went on a rent strike. Three people were killed and three policemen were wounded.

1931

Al Capone was convicted of income tax evasion on October 17 and sentenced to 11 years in prison. After serving time in several prisons, including Alcatraz, he was paroled in 1939. Suffering from tertiary syphillis, he finally died of pneumonia in his Florida home in 1947 at the age of 48.

Al's nutty as a fruitcake!

Mob bookkeeper Jake Guzik, upon hearing of Capone's
condition after his release from prison

1934

On July 22, a broiling night in the middle of a heat wave, bank robber John Dillinger went to the Biograph Theater on North Lincoln Avenue to see a movie. On his way out, he was gunned down by federal agents.

Q: What movie did Dillinger see that night?
A: *Manhattan Melodrama,* starring Clark Gable. Still operating at 2433 North Lincoln, the Biograph still runs *Manhattan Melodrama* every July 24, charging the same admission John Dillinger paid—25 cents.

Q: The FBI learned of Dillinger's presence at the Biograph through a tip-off from "The Lady in Red." What was her name and occupation?
A: Her name was Anna Sage, and she was a self-employed prostitute. Some historians doubt, incidentally, that she wore a red dress that night.

1940

On August 8 Eleanor "Blonde Tigress" Jarman escaped from the women's prison in Dwight, Illinois, where she was serving 199 years. She was never heard from again.

Q: What was her crime?
A: The diminutive Jarman, who got her name from her deftness with a blackjack, was implicated in four dozen holdups with her boyfriend, George Dale. Together they were convicted of the 1933 murder of a haberdasher named Gustav Hoch. Dale was electrocuted a year later, but Jarman, sentenced to 199 years, eluded a nationwide FBI search after her escape. No trace of her was ever found.

1956

Jack Johnson, a burly ex-marine with a heart of gold, became the youngest warden in the history of the Cook County Jail. Wanting to hide from his three daughters the full scope of his participation in executions, Johnson invented a widely believed story about there being three levers connected to the electric chair. Supposedly, three prison officials pulled the levers simultaneously without knowing which of them was making the death-dealing connection. Friendly reporters helped perpetuate the myth.

Q: Where is Cook County Jail, and how did it get there?

A: It was built in 1929 at 26th Street and California because the county already owned the land and couldn't afford any other site.

1960

When a smalltime thief named Richard Morrison was arrested, he blew the whistle on a burglary ring run by policemen. The Summerdale police scandal nearly toppled the second Daley administration, and the mayor established a blue-ribbon commission to investigate the charges.

Q: Who headed the commission?

A: Orlando Wilson, a widely respected criminologist and university professor in California.

Q: What job did Wilson get after the commission disbanded?

A: Daley hired him as Chicago's new police superintendent.

People keep asking me why don't you look the other way? But I couldn't do that.

JACK MULLER, WHO DURING 24 YEARS ON THE CHICAGO POLICE FORCE
EARNED THE SOBRIQUET "CHICAGO'S MOST HONEST COP," NEVER TOOK
A BRIBE, REPORTED EVERY WRONGDOING, AND TICKETED ALL VIOLATORS,
INCLUDING MAYOR DALEY AND GOVERNOR STRATTON.

1966

On July 14 seven nurses were murdered by a drifter named Richard Speck. He was arrested two days later amid a massive dragnet. Scheduled to die in the electric chair, Speck got life imprisonment when the Supreme Court outlawed capital punishment.

Q: Although Speck died in prison, he returned to haunt Chicagoans in 1996. How?

A: Veteran Chicago newscaster Bill Kurtis acquired videotapes showing Speck taking drugs and engaging in sex with other inmates. When the tapes were run on the evening news they provoked cries of outrage over lapses in prison security.

Q: Richard Speck's tattoo captured considerable attention. What did it say?

A: "Born to raise Hell."

1969

The trial of the Chicago Eight, the radicals indicted for conspiring to incite riots at the Democratic Convention the previous summer, began on September 24.

Q: What was the outcome of that trial?
A: After 175 contempt citations, the gagging of one defendant, Bobby Seale, and testimony from such unlikely witnesses as poet Alan Ginsberg and author Norman Mailer, the defendants were convicted. The convictions were later overturned.

Q: Did Mayor Daley ever meet the defendants?
A: Mayor Richard J. Daley did not, but his son, Mayor Richard M. Daley, met with former defendant (and California state senator) Tom Hayden in the spring of 1996 as Chicago prepared to host the Democratic National Convention once again. The meeting was reported to be cordial, and the two discussed the possibility of planting a tree together in Grant Park.

Our crime was that we were beginning to live a new and contagious lifestyle without official authorization. We were tried for being out of control.
                                                                    TOM HAYDEN

A young man like you could have a good future in our system.
            JUDGE JULIUS HOFFMAN TO DEFENDANT HAYDEN DURING THE TRIAL

1969

On December 4 the state's attorney's office raided the West Side headquarters of the Black Panther Party, killing leaders Fred Hampton and Mark Clark. Later, investigations revealed that hundreds of bullets had been fired into the house with little or no return fire. State's Attorney Edward Hanrahan, who had ordered the raid, later lost his bid for reelection.

1971

Sylvester "Two-Gun Pete" Washington, known as the deadliest cop in Chicago history, died at age 65 of natural causes. In 18 years he claimed to have made 20,000 arrests and to have killed 16 men. He wore twin .357 magnums with pearl handles. In the words of a fellow policeman, Washington "was the star of his own show."

1974

On October 26 the Puralator Security Company's vault was burglarized of $4.3 million. It remains the largest single cash theft in U.S. history.

1974

On June 19 leading mobster Sam "Momo" Giancana was shot seven times in the head while cooking sausages in the basement of his Oak Park house.

1977

On February 17, Helen Vorhees Brach, widow of the Brach candy fortune heir, checked out of the Mayo Clinic in Minnesota and was never seen again. With an estate of $45 million, she is believed to be the wealthiest person ever to have vanished without a trace.

Q: Nearly 20 years later, a man was imprisoned for conspiracy that resulted in her murder. What was his name, and why did some people doubt his guilt?
A: Richard Bailey, who had a long-standing reputation for separating women from their money in shady horse deals, was convicted after a questionable trial despite the fact that he had no demonstrable motive.

1980

On March 12 John Wayne Gacy was convicted of more murders than anyone else in U.S. history. He waited 15 years on death row until he was finally executed in 1995.

1982

Seven people died beginning September 29 from poisoned capsules of Tylenol that had been inserted into bottles before sale, leading federal authorities to later establish methods for sealing all such containers sold at retail. The murders were never solved.

1983

Three Cook County judges and seven other people were indicted on federal corruption charges after a three-year investigation known as Operation Graylord.

1990

Joseph "Pops" Panczko, dean of Chicago's trunk poppers and lock pickers, retired at the age of 72 after serving time for his 200th arrest. He had begun his career at age 12 by stealing coats from the cloak room at Humboldt Park Elementary School.

1995

Authorities estimated that of 1,050 reputed gangland hits in Chicago history, only four have been successfully prosecuted.

CHAPTER 5

Butchers Bound for Heaven

I am just a butcher trying to go to Heaven.

PHILIP DANFORTH ARMOUR, CA. 1895

For always our villains have hearts of gold, and all our heroes are slightly tainted. It always takes somebody like Hink, in whom avarice and generosity mingled like hot rum and cold water in his own Tom-and-Jerries, to run a city wherein wanton heart and freezing greed beat, like the blood and the breath, as one....

NELSON ALGREN, 1952

The flip side of the crime coin is social responsibility, and Chicago has been as innovative in the fields of social work, feminism, and vice suppression as it was in bootlegging. That these two extremes should coexist in the same time and place is testament once again to Chicago's rapid growth. Where there is fast money to be made, there will always be corruption in need of suppression.

The story of social reform in Chicago is that of a town torn between "clean-it-up" and "let it be" attitudes. Religion has played a big role in this struggle, most notably in the silent tug of war between Catholics and Protestants. Catholics, especially ethnic groups such as the Irish and Germans, have historically viewed taverns as part of community life, while Protestants have tended to regard them as dens of depravity. Time and again, Chicago has been the battleground for these two opposing views of humanity and society. If the last chapter paid attention to some of Chicago's most infamous moments, this chapter will pay homage to some of its most glorious.

1816

Chicago's first organized school opened its doors to seven children in a log building donated by John Kinzie. The first public school was established 17 years later by Miss Eliza Chappel.

1837

The first medical school in Chicago was chartered. Named after Dr. Benjamin Rush, a physician who signed the Declaration of Independence, it survives today as Rush-Presbyterian-St. Luke's Hospital.

Q: Early records indicate that Chicago had only six physicians to serve a population of 4,500. By comparison, how many lawyers did it have?
A: Twenty-seven.

Q: Rush Medical College was the first school in the country to award a medical degree to a black man, David Jones Peck. How is he remembered today?
A: The CTA station near Rush-Presbyterian-St. Luke's Hospital is dedicated to Dr. Peck.

1846

St. Xavier's Academy for young women was opened by the Sisters of Mercy in 1846. It is still operating today as St. Xavier University on the South Side.

1847

The American Medical Association was founded in Chicago, which is still its national headquarters.

Q: In 1850 the Chicago Medical Society was founded by a man who not only became its first president but who, as mayor, instigated the Beer Hall Riots, one of the city's most colorful insurrections. Who was he?
A: Dr. Levi Boone who, as mayor in 1855, enforced an ordinance calling for taverns to close on Sundays. A protest march organized by German immigrants soon turned into a riot that ended with one man killed and several wounded.

1847

Chicago's first law school was opened by John J. Brown.

1849

The Chicago Orphan Asylum opened with W. H. Brown as president.

1850

Chicago's first hospital opened. Called the Illinois General Hospital of the Lake, it was located at Rush and North Water Streets. Most medicine was still practiced by means of house calls, fees for which were $1.50 for a day house call and $3.00 for a night call (10:00 P.M. to daybreak).

1851

The Chicago Lunatic asylum had 22 patients under the care of a Dr. Mead.

1851

Chicago got its first institution of higher learning when Northwestern University was organized at the Clark Street Methodist Church. A $1,200 salary was approved to hire a president, but two years went by before the position was filled—by Clark Titus Hinman.

Q: Why are most Evanstonians familiar with Hinman's name?
A: Hinman Avenue is a major downtown thoroughfare.

1855

At Northwestern University, two professors began offering classes to 10 students.

1855

Both the Chicago Theological Seminary and the Chicago Phrenological Society were organized.

Q: What is phrenology?
A: A now discredited belief that the shape of the head influenced behavior.

1855

School inspectors published a rule allowing Scriptures to be read in the morning exercises without comment.

1856

The Chicago Relief and Aid Society was formed by the city's Protestant elite. Believing that poverty was the result of a character flaw, its founders asked the poor to show virtuous behavior before receiving any assistance.

1857

On January 27 the Chicago Temperance Society was formed to encourage total abstinence.

Q: Attitudes among Christians toward alcohol split heavily along denominational lines. How?
A: The temperance movement has always been led by Protestants. Catholics, especially ethnic Catholics such as the Irish and the Austrians, have traditionally been "wets."

1857

Rev. Arnold Damen established the Holy Family Free School for Girls in his parish—the first parochial parish school in Chicago. Construction began on Holy Family Church, at 12th Street and Morgan. It was then called the church on the prairie because it seemed so far out of town.

Q: What other school did Damen help found, and when?
A: St. Ignatius College, the forerunner to both Loyola University and St. Ignatius Prep, was established in 1870.

Q: How is Damen remembered today?
A: Damen Avenue, a major north-south boulevard, was named after him.

1858

Bishop O'Regan of Chicago tried to extend the reach of the Chicago diocese when he traveled to St. Anne in Kankakee County for the purpose of excommunicating renegade Father Chiniquy. Chiniquy retaliated by becoming a Presbyterian.

1858

Chicago's YMCA was organized with 151 initial members.

1859

The Chicago College of Pharmacy was established, the first of its kind in the country. It later became part of the University of Illinois.

1859

The Sisters of Mercy opened the Magdalene Asylum for women who wished to abandon a life of degradation but who had no means of honest support.

1860

Three years before the Emancipation Proclamation, the Chicago Board of Education voted to admit a black girl to the normal department of the high school.

1863

Dr. Mary Harris Thompson, Chicago's first female surgeon, opened the Chicago Hospital for Women and Children.

Q: The Chicago Hospital for Women and Children was all but which of the following?

1. The first women's medical college in the Midwest.
2. The first nursing school in Chicago.
3. Chicago's first lying-in hospital.
4. The first cancer detection station in the Midwest.
5. The first mental hygiene clinic for working women.

A: All but number 3.

1863

Mary Livermore and Jane Hoge organized the Great Northwestern Sanitary Fair to raise funds for the U.S. Sanitary Commission, which had as its mission the relief of wounded and imprisoned Civil War soldiers.

Q: Where was the Sanitary Fair held?
A: It was in a hastily constructed exhibition hall in what is now Grant Park.

Q: What social cause did Mary Livermore turn to when the war was over?
A: Women's rights. In 1869, she founded *The Agitator*, the first periodical devoted to women's suffrage.

1864

Teachers were forbidden by the Board of Education to discuss sectarian issues or party politics in school.

1869

Myra Bradwell, who organized the Midwest's first suffrage convention, became the first female lawyer in Illinois. Her first application had been rejected.

The court ... [denies] ... our application for a license ... by reason of the disability imposed by your married condition—it being assumed you are a married woman.
ILLINOIS SUPREME COURT'S DECISION ON MYRA BRADWELL'S
FIRST APPLICATION TO PRACTICE LAW

Q: Twenty years later, Bradwell finally was admitted to the bar in recognition of all but which of the following?

1. Establishing the Chicago Legal News.
2. Establishing the Women's Bar Association.
3. Founding the Illinois Industrial School for Girls.
4. Encouraging a group of male lawyers to found the Chicago Bar Association.

A: Number 2. The Woman's Bar Association wasn't established until 1914, 20 years after Bradwell's death.

1871

The infant mortality rate in Chicago among children five years and younger was 70.7 percent.

1872

Henry Demarest Lloyd, a lawyer turned social reformer, joined the *Chicago Tribune* and proceeded to attack large corporations, especially the Standard Oil Company.

Q: In 1873 Lloyd married Jessie Bross, the daughter of *Tribune* publisher and chief Chicago booster William Bross. Twenty years later, a difference over what issue led Bross to disinherit his daughter?
A: When in 1893 Lloyd, with his wife's support, asked Governor John Peter Altgeld to pardon the Haymarket martyrs, Bross disowned her.

Q: In 1899 Lloyd wrote *Wealth Against Commonwealth* and actively supported labor causes around the country. His home became a gathering place for many reformers, from Jane Addams to Booker T. Washington. What was his home called, and where was it located?

A: Called Wayside, it still stands on Sheridan Road and Lloyd Place in Winnetka. A park across the street is named after the Lloyds.

1874

The Women's Christian Temperance Union was founded in Evanston. Frances E. Willard was the first president.

Q: Why did the WCTU get its start in Chicago?
A: Protestant reformers had made Chicago the center of the national temperance movement even as the predominantly Catholic politicians kept it a "wet" town—a contemporary survey reported that Chicago had one saloon for every 26 men.

Q: Where are the WCTU's headquarters today?
A: Still in Evanston's, at 1730 Chicago Avenue, right behind the restored home of Frances Willard.

1876

The City of Chicago's Department of Health was established.

1879

Rev. David Swing, minister of the Fourth Presbyterian Church, was tried for heresy. The popular pastor had raised the ire of national Presbyterian leaders by preaching that Christianity should be relevant to everyday life. Even though he was acquitted, Swing left Fourth Presbyterian and started the non-denominational Central Church at State and Randolph Streets, taking many parishioners with him.

Q: Where were the First, Second, and Third Presbyterian churches located?
A: The Second Presbyterian Church was built at 1936 South Michigan Avenue by parishioners who left First Presbyterian in a dispute over abolition. The Second was—and remains—a handsome landmark edifice designed by James Renwick, architect of New York's St. Patrick's Church. Records indicate that no Third Presbyterian was ever formed.

1880

Rabbi Emil Hirsch became head of the Sinai Congregation and began holding Jewish Sabbath services on Sundays.

Q: Hirsch became well known for other controversial moves. Which of the following did he not do?

1. Invite Jane Addams and fellow social reformer Hannah Solomon to speak in temple at a time when women still sat separately from the men.
2. Have his brother-in-law, Dankmar Adler, design his congregation's new temple.
3. Suggest establishing a settlement house for millionaires' sons on the grounds that they were often more ignorant than the children of working men.
4. Become the first American rabbi to teach at a secular university when he joined the faculty at the University of Chicago.

A: Number 2. Adler's father had been an early rabbi of K.A.M. Isaiah Israel, Chicago's oldest Jewish congregation, and Adler and Sullivan received a commission to design its temple. The building still stands today as the Pilgrim Baptist Church at 3301 South Indiana Avenue.

1881

The family of Michael Reese established a hospital in his name. Over the next century, it would become one of the city's largest and most important medical centers.

Q: The original building still stands. Where is it?
A: Originally a 60-bed facility, the brick structure is at Ellis Avenue and 22nd Street.

1884

Cyrus McCormick Jr. succeeded his father as head of McCormick Reaper Works. Barely out of his teens, he was in over his head. One of his first actions was to cut wages and fire highly skilled workers. Some historians attribute his moves to the family's desire to raise money for the McCormick Theological Seminary.

1885

McCormick's actions helped usher in a 10-year period of labor unrest in Chicago. On Thanksgiving Day several thousand workers marched down Prairie Avenue, where Chicago's business elite lived. Their goal was to ruin the digestions of the rich and, by all reports, they succeeded.

Q: Who led the protesters?
A: Albert Parsons, who was later hanged after the Haymarket Riot, and his wife, Lucy.

1886

The Haymarket Riot occurred. Another strike at the McCormick plant led workers to rally in the Haymarket on May 4 to hear speakers, including Albert Parsons. Mayor Carter Harrison was in the crowd and ordered police to stay away from the gathering. After his departure the police, led by Captain John Bonfield, marched on the protesters. A bomb was thrown, and seven policemen and one bystander were killed.

> *We suggest ... that [corporate leaders] keep a close watch for designing men who are influencing their employees to join these organizations and eventually cause a strike.*
> FROM A LETTER CIRCULATED BY THE PINKERTON DETECTIVE AGENCY IN 1885

After a patently unfair trial seven protesters were sentenced to death and one to fifteen years in prison. On November 11, 1887, four of the men—August Spies, Albert Parsons, George Engel, and Adolph Fischer—were hanged. Four days earlier, Louis Lingg, one of the condemned, had cheated the gallows by biting a percussion cap. In 1893 the remaining men were pardoned by Governor John Peter Altgeld.

> *There will come a time when our silence will be more powerful than the voices you hear today.*
> AUGUST SPIES ON HIS WAY TO THE GALLOWS

> *It is shown that various attempts were made to bring to justice the men who wore the uniform of the law while violating it, but all to no avail.... The laboring people found the prisons always open to them.*
> JOHN PETER ALTGELD

1886

Some 5,000 cases of typhoid were reported in one year. Five years later, typhoid killed 10,000 Chicagoans.

Q: How did Chicago finally get typhoid under control?
A: By reversing the flow of the Chicago River. Chicago's typhoid was spread mainly through drinking lake water contaminated by sewage from the river.

1889

Dwight L. Moody established the Chicago Bible Institute to train fellow evangelists. He'd arrived in Chicago 30 years earlier as a street-corner preacher.

Q: Nelson Algren, no friend of organized religion, nonetheless immortalized Moody's most famous line as a chapter title in *City on the Make*. What was it?

A: "Are you a Christian?" which, according to legend, Moody asked over and over as he wandered the city's poorer districts.

Q: How is Moody remembered in Chicago today?

A: In two noted institutions. The Moody Church stands at the triple intersection of North Avenue and Clark and LaSalle Streets. The Moody Bible Institute, which he founded, took his name after Moody's death in 1899. Its main campus is today located along LaSalle Street north of Chicago Avenue.

Character is what a man is in the dark.

DWIGHT L. MOODY

1889

On September 18 Chicago's most famous monument to social work and the progressive spirit, Hull House, was opened by Jane Addams and Ellen Gates Starr.

Q: How did Hull House get its name?

A: Initially it was located in a single building that had once been the home of Charles J. Hull, a real estate developer. The building still stands at 800 South Halsted Street and is open to the public as a museum.

Q: Where did Addams and Starr get the idea for Hull House?

A: During a trip to Europe they had visited Toynbee House, a settlement house in the Whitechapel district of London—the same district where Jack the Ripper had carried out his gruesome attacks a few years earlier.

Q: How many settlement houses were there in Chicago?

A: Hull House was by no means unique. By 1911 the city boasted 36 such establishments, the most famous others being Chicago Commons and University House.

Q: Social work took many forms at Hull House. What world-famous musician first played in a Hull House band?

A: Benny Goodman.

1890

Holy Family became the largest English-speaking parish in the entire United States, serving 25,000 people.

Q: By the turn of the century, Chicago had become the largest Catholic archdiocese in the United States. When was the first Mass celebrated there, and by whom?

A: In 1674 by Father Jacques Marquette at what is now the intersection of Damen Avenue and the South Branch of the Chicago River.

Q: As recently as 1990, Holy Family attracted considerable attention. Why?

A: When the Archdiocese of Chicago ordered the deteriorating church demolished, a group of people organized a national campaign to raise $1 million to save the historic building. They succeeded.

1892

Popular preacher Rev. Frank Gunsaulus preached a sermon entitled "What I Would Do If I Had a Million Dollars" at Plymouth Congregational Church. Among his suggestions was starting a school to convert poor boys into engineers. Meatpacker Philip D. Armour was in the congregation and promptly pledged that sum to start a school if Gunsaulus would become its president.

Q: What school was thus founded?

A: The Armour Institute, which later became Illinois Institute of Technology.

Q: Gunsaulus is remembered today principally for a hall named after him. Where is it?

A: It connects the east and west sides of the Art Institute of Chicago.

Q: The Armour family was responsible for several other benevolences. Name some.

A: The Armour Mission on 31st Street was one of the first settlement houses to serve Chicago's Negro community. Armour Flats was a nearby subsidized housing project.

The millionaire's daughter and my lady's dressmaker or laundry woman are already standing there, shoulder to shoulder, learning to see things from the same point of view.

PHILIP D. ARMOUR

1892

William Rainey Harper started the University of Chicago. Ever the entrepreneur, Harper relied on financial backing from John D. Rockefeller and many Chicago millionaires to raid eastern schools and provide the new university with a distinguished faculty even before it opened.

1893

Chicago's first open heart surgery was performed by Daniel Hale Williams on a street fighter.

Q: What made Dr. Williams's accomplishment even more significant?
A: He was an African-American surgeon at a time when there were very few of them.

Q: Williams was also instrumental in establishing a major Chicago Hospital. What was it, and why was it significant?
A: Provident Hospital was the first hospital in the city to admit Negro patients.

1893

Thorton Chase, a Chicago insurance salesman, became the first American to join the Baha'i religion.

Q: Why is Chicago important to the Baha'i faith today?
A: The Baha'i Temple in Wilmette, 10 miles north of Chicago, is one of only a half dozen such temples in the world.

1893

During the World's Parliament of Religions held as part of the Columbian Exposition, Hannah Greenebaum Solomon organized the National Council of Jewish Women and served as its president for the next 12 years.

1894

Sociology was invented at the University Settlement House by Mary McDowell.

Q: Where did McDowell locate her settlement house?
A: In the poor Back of the Yards neighborhood on the near South Side, where most stockyard workers lived.

Q: Mary McDowell had a nickname that stemmed from her efforts to clean up the branch of the Chicago River that went through the stockyards. What was it?

A: The Duchess of Bubbly Creek.

1894

Graham Taylor established Chicago Commons Settlement House, which a century later operates seven beneficent centers in Chicago and a summer camp in Michigan.

Q: Though never a faculty member, Taylor established what school within the University of Chicago?

A: The School of Civics and Philanthropy, now known as the School of Social Service Administration.

Q: One of the early teachers at the School of Civics and Philanthropy was also the first woman to receive a law degree from the University of Chicago. Who was she?

A: Sophinisba P. Breckinridge.

1896

The Laboratory School at the University of Chicago was established by philosophy professor John Dewey to teach cooperative learning instead of sheer memorization.

Q: What other Chicago secondary school was founded along the same principles?

A: Parker School on the North Side was started by Colonel Francis Parker, creator of the normal school idea for the training of teachers. It was financed principally by Anita McCormick Blaine, daughter of the reaper king.

1896

On January 29 Dr. Emil H. Grubbe was the first to use an x-ray for the treatment of a disease when he treated a woman suffering from recurring breast cancer with his own, primitively designed x-ray device.

1898

Dr. Frank Billings, a professor at Rush Medical College, and William Rainey Harper, president of the University of Chicago, effected a merger between the two institutions and created the Medical School at the University of Chicago.

Q: Billings had become a friend of Chicago's elite by doing what?
A: He was the physician who made house calls on affluent Prairie Avenue.

Q: For a physician, Billings died in a rather ignominious way. What was it?
A: At the age of 78 he slipped on a rug in his home and died from internal bleeding.

1899

Chicago was the first American city to establish a juvenile court.

Q: A Chicago social reformer was prominent in the creation not only of the juvenile court but of the Juvenile Protective Association. She also endowed a summer camp for underprivileged children. What was her name?
A: Louise DeKoven Bowen. Her grandmother had been the first child born at Fort Dearborn.

1900

Margaret Haley was elected an officer in the Chicago Teachers Federation, one of the many labor and professional groups to grow out of the World's Columbian Exposition. She soon became the nation's leading advocate of professional treatment for schoolteachers.

1902

Chicago's most famous preacher, Rev. William Ashley Sunday, better known as Billy Sunday, was ordained. An evangelist as popular in his own day as Billy Graham was a half century later, Sunday drew immense crowds. He once preached to starving miners in Colorado that their poverty was caused by their drinking, and he later became a major figure in the prohibition movement.

*The stockyards' owners imported Billy Sunday to divert their underpaid
hunkies from going on strike by shouting them dizzy with God.*
                                                        BEN HECHT

Q: What song immortalized Billy Sunday?
A: The song "Chicago" refers to "the town Billy Sunday could not shut down."

Q: What did Billy Sunday do before he became a minister, and what made him change his career?

A: He was a baseball player with the Chicago White Stockings. He "found the light" after hearing hymns at the Pacific Garden Mission.

1905

The Industrial Workers of the World, the IWW, or simply "the Wobblies" was formed in Chicago by "Big Bill" Haywood, Lucy Parsons, "Mother" Jones, and Eugene Debs, among others. The IWW enjoyed a brief surge of political strength just prior to World War I but was finally overwhelmed by a combination of big businessmen, politicians, policemen, judges, and self-styled patriots, who found its "one union" message socialistic.

Q: Where is the headquarters of the IWW today?
A: It remained in Chicago until 1989, when it was moved to California and, later, to Ypsilanti, Michigan.

Q: Lucy Parsons and Eugene Debs had already played significant roles in Chicago labor history. What were they?
A: Lucy Parsons and her husband, Albert, had participated in the Haymarket protest, for which he was later hanged. Debs had been the leader of the American Railway Union during the Pullman Strike.

1908

The first commercial use of chlorine to treat sewage was tried in Chicago.

1909

Grace Abbott, director of the Chicago Immigrants Protective League, pressured the city government to pass a law against unscrupulous practices in the employment of immigrants.

Q: What were Grace Abbott's two connections with the University of Chicago?
A: She got a Ph.D. in political science there in 1908, and her sister Edith taught at the university's School of Social Work.

1909

Ella Flagg Young became the first female superintendent of public schools in Chicago. Although 64 years old at the time, she was a dynamic leader who instituted vocational courses in the high schools and advocated courses in ethics and morality.

Q: Which of the following other firsts did Young not achieve?

1. The first female Ph.D. from the School of Education at the University of Chicago.
2. The first woman to attain the rank of full professor there.
3. The first female president of the Illinois Teachers Association.
4. The first woman to hold a cabinet seat.
5. The first woman to receive an honorary doctorate from the University of Illinois.

A: All but number 4. Though she was in Washington, D.C., on a speaking tour when she died at age 73, she was never part of a national administration.

Those who live in the mountain have a longer day than those who live in the valley. Sometimes all we need to brighten our day is to climb a little higher.
                                        ELLA FLAGG YOUNG

1910

Abraham Flexner wrote his famed Flexner Report, a study of medical education in the United States. Of Chicago he said, "The city of Chicago is in respect to medical education the plague spot of the country." He charged that some of Chicago's medical schools were merely commercial diploma mills, turning out uneducated and ill-trained practitioners.

Q: Fifty years later, Chicago could claim a different reputation in the field of medical education. What was it?
A: With five renowned medical schools, three dental schools, and the nation's first pharmacy school, Chicago replaced Vienna as the world center for medical training. At that time roughly one-fifth of all American doctors received some part of their medical education in Chicago.

1910

Ida B. Wells, the daughter of Mississippi slaves, formed the Negro Fellowship League on the South Side to provide social services to Negroes newly arrived from the South.

Q: Ida B. Wells was a leader in the movement to promote racial integration. She was also responsible for all but which of the following?

1. She sued the Chesapeake & Ohio Railroad when the conductor ordered her to sit in the "colored section."

2. She attacked city officials in a scathing 81-page booklet entitled *Why the Colored American Is Not in the World's Columbian Exposition.*
3. She sponsored the building of a South Side housing project.
4. She married Ferdinand L. Barnett, the first black Cook County assistant state's attorney and a newspaper publisher.
5. She served as a probation officer of the Chicago Municipal Court.

A: All but number 3. The Ida B. Wells Homes were named after her but were built in the 1950s across from the house she had shared with Barnett.

1911

DePaul University became the first Roman Catholic university in the United States to go coeducational.

1912

Following in the footsteps of David Swing, Rev. Preston Bradley was charged with heresy for preaching that baptism is not required for salvation. Bradley quit the Presbyterian Church and founded the Peoples Church of Chicago, an unorthodox congregation that eventually numbered some 4,000 parishioners.

Q: Where was—and is—the Peoples Church located?
A: In the Uptown area, at 941 West Lawrence Avenue.

Q: The Peoples Church was the first Chicago church to do what?
A: Regularly broadcast services on the radio.

> *I am not orthodox about anything. I am thoroughly, completely, adequately, gloriously, and triumphantly a heretic.*
>
> REV. PRESTON BRADLEY

Q: The opinionated Bradley—he advocated birth control when the subject was still taboo and attacked the Ku Klux Klan and anti-Semitism at a time when both were tolerated—is best memorialized today in one of Chicago's most glorious public spaces. What and where is it?
A: Preston Bradley Hall in the Chicago Cultural Center is today the site of free concerts every Wednesday at noon and numerous other activities.

1916

Three people died and scores became sick at a dinner honoring George Mundelein's elevation to archbishop of Chicago. It was later discovered that the soup had been poisoned by an atheist.

1917

St. Francis Xavier Cabrini died in Columbus Hospital after founding 70 hospitals, schools and orphanages, and inducting over 4,000 women into her Missionary Sisters of the Sacred Heart. In 1947 she was canonized, thus becoming the first American saint.

I can do all things in Him Who is my strength.
                                                ST. FRANCIS XAVIER CABRINI

1917

Dr. Ben Reitman grew up among the bordellos on South Clark Street, became Emma Goldman's lover, was imprisoned for advocating birth control, and was known for his work among the homeless.

Q: Reitman eventually became a city health official. Who hired him and what were his duties?
A: Dr. John Dill Robertson hired Reitman to work among Chicago's hobo population.

A tramp is a man who doesn't work, who apparently doesn't want to work, who lives without working, and is constantly traveling. A hobo is a nonskilled, nonemployed laborer without money, looking for work. A beggar is a man who hangs around a low class saloon and begs or earns a few pennies a day in order to obtain work. He is usually an inebriate.
                                                DR. BEN REITMAN

1918

G. C. Searle and Company, newly located in Chicago, began mass-producing Dr. Ehrlich's "Magic Bullet" to battle syphilis.

1920

The city's first allergy clinic opened at Rush Hospital.

1923

Mary Bartelme became the first woman judge in Illinois history and the second in the nation. She was known especially for her work with children, serving first as Cook County public guardian and later as an assistant judge in Juvenile Court.

Q: What social institution still exists in Chicago that is a tribute to Bartelme?
A: In 1913 Bartelme established what were called "Mary Clubs" for young or homeless girls. The Mary Bartelme Homes still serve the same population.

There are no bad children. There are confused, neglected children, love-starved and resentful children, and what they need most I try to give them—understanding, and a fresh start in the right direction.
MARY BARTELME

1925

Chicago had a total of 14,956 hospital beds.

1926

The First Eucharistic Congress to be held in the United States met in Chicago at Soldier Field.

1929

Robert Maynard Hutchins was elected president of the University of Chicago. Only 30 years old, he was the youngest man ever to head a major American university.

Q: What curricular reform was Hutchins most famous for?
A: Introducing the *Great Books of the Western World,* the same canon promoted years later by University of Chicago Professor Allan Bloom in *The Closing of the American Mind.*

1939

Having survived the poison attack, George Cardinal Mundelein was the first Chicago cardinal to vote in a Papal election.

Q: George Cardinal Mundelein was the youngest monsignor and the youngest auxiliary bishop in American history. How old was he when he became archbishop of Chicago, and how long did he hold that post?
A: He was only 43 at the time and served as archbishop for 24 years.

Q: Name two Chicago institutions named after Mundelein.
A: Mundelein College (now part of Loyola University) and St. Mary of the Lake Seminary, around which the town bearing Mundelein's name soon grew.

Hitler is nothing but an Austrian paperhanger and a poor one at that.
GEORGE CARDINAL MUNDELEIN

1939

Baxter Laboratories introduced the "closed system" of blood banking. This was the first time blood was collected, stored for up to three weeks, and then given to a patient without the blood ever coming in contact with the outside air.

1939

Saul Alinsky and Joseph Meegan formed the Back of the Yards Neighborhood Council, one of Chicago's—and the nation's—most famous community activist organizations. Ill-mannered and aggressive though he was, Alinsky got results.

Q: What other famous Chicago community groups did Alinsky start?
A: The Industrial Areas Foundation, designed to help a broad variety of workers, and The Woodlawn Organization (T.W.O.), which attacked white slumlords in black neighborhoods.

Q: Two of Alinksy's books are considered the ultimate how-to manuals for community organizers. What are their names, and when did they come out?
A: *Reveille for Radicals* (1945) and *Rules for Radicals* (1971).

If the end doesn't justify the means, what the hell does?… The meatpacking industry has never been able to distinguish between a Hereford steer and a human being.… Change comes from power, and power comes from organiza-tion.… In order to act, people must get together.
SAUL ALINSKY

1942

On December 2 Manhattan Project scientists, working under Stagg Field at the University of Chicago, achieved the world's first self-sustaining nuclear reaction—in popular parlance, they "split the atom." The project team was led by immigrant and Nobel laureate Enrico Fermi.

When do we get scared?
ENRICO FERMI, AS THE FINAL CADMIUM RODS WERE
WITHDRAWN TO SET OFF THE CHAIN REACTION

Q: Who was the first American to win a Nobel Prize, when, and in what field?

A: Albert Abraham Michelson of the University of Chicago won it for physics in 1907.

Q: All told, how many people associated with the University of Chicago have won Nobel Prizes?

A: Sixty-seven, more than any other institution in the world.

Q: In what field have University of Chicagoans won the most Nobel Prizes, and how many?

A: The Nobel Prize for physics has gone to 23 University of Chicago faculty members.

Q: In what field have University of Chicagoans won more Nobel Prizes than any other university, and how many?

A: In economics, and the number is 16.

Q: How many University of Chicagoans have won the Nobel Prize since 1990?

A: Nine. Paul Crutzen and E. Sherwood Rowland in 1995 for chemistry, Merton H. Miller and Harry M. Markowitz in 1990, Ronald H. Chase in 1991, Gary S. Becker in 1992, Robert W. Fogel in 1993, and Robert E. Lucas Jr. in 1995, all for economics; and Jerome I. Friedman in 1990 for physics.

Q: Two Chicagoans have won the Nobel Peace Prize. Who were they, when did they win them, and for what?

A: Charles Gates Dawes won it in 1925 for his work in helping to rebuild Europe after World War I, and Jane Addams won it in 1931 for her pioneering work at Hull House.

Q: How many Chicagoans have won the Nobel Prize for literature?

A: Two. Ernest Hemingway (born and raised in Oak Park) in 1954, and Saul Bellow in 1976.

1950

In a survey 45 percent of Chicago's medical doctors said they were in general practice.

1953

Amino acids were discovered at the University of Chicago by Dr. Stanley Miller.

1954

Chicago had 23 theological seminaries—Catholic, Jewish, and Protestant—twice the number of its closest competitor, New York City.

1954

On August 15 more than 125,000 Chicagoans attended the Festival of Faith in Soldier Field, held as part of the World Council of Churches Assembly in Evanston. It was the world's largest such gathering until the World Congress of Churches held a 100th anniversary gathering in 1993, also in Chicago.

1975

J. Allen Hynek, an astronomer at Northwestern University, formed the Center for UFO Studies, insisting that the possibility of UFOs be taken seriously.

Q: What famous phrase did Hynek invent, and where was it popularized?
A: "Close encounter." Steven Spielberg took the term for his 1977 movie, *Close Encounters of the Third Kind,* in which Hynek himself played a cameo role.

1976

The Uses of Enchantment, a seminal study on the psychological meanings in fairy tales, was published by Dr. Bruno Bettelheim of the University of Chicago. It won a National Book Award for its author.

Q: Bettelheim also founded a school in Chicago known particularly for its treatment of autistic children. What and where is it?
A: The Sonia Shankman Orthogenic School is part of the University of Chicago.

1982

Joseph Cardinal Bernardin was appointed archbishop of Chicago, succeeding John Cardinal Cody, who died amid scandals over financial misappropriations.

1985

The largest hospital in the country was Cook County Hospital, with over 4,500 beds.

1989

The Chicago Public School system became the first urban system in the country to return control to local school councils.

Q: What now universal reform did the Chicago Public Schools make 120 years earlier?

A: With school enrollments doubling every three years in the 1860s, School Superintendent William Wells divided the schools into grades to give teachers better control.

1992

Provident Hospital, established a century earlier by Dr. Daniel Hale Williams to serve the city's black population, reopened as part of Cook County Hospital. It had been shuttered for a decade.

CHAPTER 6

Getting the Word Out

It isn't hard to love a town for its broad and bending boulevards, its lamplit parks and its endowed opera. But you can never truly love a place till you love it for its alleys, too. For the horse-and-wagon, cat-and-ash-can alleys below the thousand-girded El.

NELSON ALGREN, CITY ON THE MAKE

I don't need nobody to tell me about newspapers. I've been a newspaperman for fifteen years. A cross between a bootlegger and a whore. And if you want to know something, you'll all end up on the copy desk—grey-headed, humpbacked slobs, dodging garnishees when you're ninety!

BEN HECHT AND CHARLES MACARTHUR,
The Front Page

Chicago has always been a tough town for writers—its obsession with commerce and politics both attracts and repels them. It's an aphorism that a great writer can leave Chicago and no one notices, while another great writer can arrive here to similarly empty acclaim. Chicago is not, on the surface, a literary place.

Yet Chicago has left a profound mark on the literary world of America. The essential feature of American writing is realism, and Chicago has produced some of the grittiest, down-lowest realism ever written. Many of this country's greatest journalists have worked on Chicago newspapers, many of the most quintessential American novels have been written in, or about, Chicago, and a raft of films and television shows have glorified Chicago as well.

Nelson Algren found Chicago compelling while *New Yorker* writer A. J. Liebling found it so wanting, he dubbed it the "Second City." But none of the writers who have sojourned here have found Chicago neutral. Love it or hate it, Chicago got into their fevered bloodstreams and helped them write great words that live today, long after most of them have gone on to the Great City Desk in the Sky.

1833

The *Chicago Democrat,* the city's first newspaper, published its first issue in November, reporting that the village trustees had made it illegal for a hog to run the streets without a ring in its nose.

1845

The first foreign language newspaper to be published in Chicago, the *Chicago Volksfreund,* appeared in November.

1856

The first novel set in Chicago was published. Called *Wau-Bun: Early Days of the Northwest,* it was written by Juliette Magill Kinzie, a pioneer settler, along with her husband, John Harris Kinzie. The novel romanticized the heroism of her father-in-law, the original John Kinzie, during the days of Fort Dearborn.

1856

The *Prairie Farmer,* Chicago's first periodical, became a weekly and enlarged its format.

1861

Wilber F. Storey purchased the *Chicago Times* from Cyrus McCormick and quickly turned it into a sensational tabloid. Its "yellow journalism" sold so well that by the time of the Great Fire, the *Times* was the Midwest's leading newspaper.

Q: What was the motto of the *Chicago Times* under Storey's editorship?
A: "To print the news and raise hell!"

1873

The Chicago Public Library opened in an old water tank at LaSalle and Adams Streets. The basis of its collection was 8,000 volumes collected by popular English writer Thomas Hughes *(Tom Brown's School Days)* and sent to Chicago after the Great Fire.

Q: How is Hughes remembered today at the Chicago Public Library?
A: The children's library at the Harold Washington Library Center is named after him.

1875

The *Chicago Daily News* was founded on Christmas Day. Publisher Melville E. Stone, a staunch opponent of yellow journalism, promised that the "paper would be candid, comprehensive, concise, clean, and cheap."

Q: What distinguished the *News* from its competitors?
A: Along with good writing, the *News* was Chicago's first penny newspaper, a price that greatly widened its circle of readers.

Q: Who was the *Daily News* publisher during Stone's editorship?
A: Victor Lawson.

Q: Name three noted talents whom Lawson hired.
A: Cartoonist John T. McCutcheon and columnists George Ade and Eugene Field.

Q: As a publisher Lawson is remembered for all but one of the following:

1. Printing the newspaper's circulation figures.
2. Running full-page ads.
3. Using newsboys as selling agents.
4. Establishing the City News Bureau and the Associated Press.

A: All but number 4. Lawson established the Chicago City Press Association, forerunner of the City News Bureau, and the Associated Press was established long before Lawson got into the newspaper business. He was, however, its president from 1894 to 1900 and served on its board until his death in 1925.

1878

Lawyer Ferdinand L. Barnett founded *The Conservator,* Chicago's first black newspaper.

Q: Who was the best-known contributor to *The Conservator?*
A: Ida B. Wells, the black suffragette and staunch integrationist who was also Barnett's wife.

1883

Eugene Field, a 33-year-old St. Louis man who had worked on newspapers in Denver and Kansas City, joined the staff of the *Chicago Daily News*. Through his column—the first daily newspaper column in American history—Field became the first Chicago journalist to establish a national reputation.

Q: What was the name of the column?
A: "Sharps and Flats," and it reflected Field's wide-ranging humanitarian interests. Legend has it that Field hung around all day talking with people, then at three in the afternoon he retreated into his office, removed his jacket and shoes, and without fail produced a finished piece by six P.M.

Q: In 1883 the Saints and Sinners Club became a legendary part of Chicago literature. What was it and where did it meet?
A: More a subject of Field's imagination than an actual organization, the Saints and Sinners Club was a group of bibliophiles who hung around the rare-book corner of McClurg's Bookstore at Wabash Avenue and Monroe Street.

Q: For what is Eugene Field best remembered today?
A: Writing children's poems, including "Winken, Blinken, and Nod" and the "Little Boy Blue."

Q: Verses from two of Field's poems are carved on a statue to his memory located near a place in the city that is popular with parents and children. Where is it?
A: In Lincoln Park Zoo near the Small Mammal House.

Q: Field died in 1895, shortly before his 45th birthday, and was buried in an elegant English-style churchyard on the North Shore. What is the name of place?
A: Field was initially buried in Graceland Cemetery, but in 1926 his remains were moved to the Church of the Holy Comforter in Kenilworth.

1886

With the establishment of the Charles H. Kerr Company, Chicago became the center for leftist publishing in the English-speaking world. Kerr published works by leading radicals, a tradition it maintains today from its office in Rogers Park.

Q: Which one of the following turn-of-the-century figures wasn't published by Kerr?

1. Eugene Debs.
2. William "Big Bill" Haywood.
3. Clarence Darrow.
4. Carl Sandburg.
5. Robert Cowdrey.

A: Number 5, Robert Cowdrey. Though not well known today, Cowdrey was widely read a century ago, and he was published by the F. H. Schulz Company, another Chicago publisher specializing in leftist writers. His novel *A Tramp in Society* appeared in 1891. In 1892 Schulz also published Hamlin Garland's *A Member of the Third House,* an attack on the railroads.

Q: Why was so much radical publishing emanating from Chicago?
A: Demographics and economics. Chicago was growing rapidly, especially its immigrant population, and Europeans were already acquainted with radical politics. The exploding economic growth of Chicago also underscored the social problems that were an inevitable by product of industrialization.

1890

George Ade arrived in Chicago from Indiana and soon began producing a popular column called "Stories of the Streets and Town," illustrated by his college chum John T. McCutcheon. Like Eugene Field and Finley Peter Dunne, Ade wrote in the everyday language of ordinary people, establishing Chicago as a center of vernacular journalism. Eventually his breezy morality tales called "Fables in Slang" were made into silent films, winning him fame and fortune and enabling him to retire early to his farm in Indiana.

Early to bed, early to rise and you'll meet very few of our best people.
GEORGE ADE

Q: Which Pulitzer Prize-winning cartoonist roomed with fellow Hoosier George Ade and then married architect Howard Van Doren Shaw's daughter, Evelyn?
A: John T. McCutcheon, best known for his "Injun Summer" cartoon, which the *Tribune* reprinted every fall for nearly three-quarters of a century.

1890

Chicago earned its most famous nickname not—as many people believe—from its climate but from its braggadocio. During the competition to secure the proposed 1893 world's fair, Charles Gibson Dana of the *New York Sun* cautioned his readers to "pay no attention to the claims of the Windy City" who "couldn't build a World's Fair if they won it."

1891

Carter H. Harrison's two novellas, *A Summer's Outing* and *The Old Man's Story,* made him the only mayor of Chicago to publish works of fiction.

1892

Francis Fisher Browne and William Morton Payne took over publication of *The Dial,* and turned it into the leading literary criticism journal in the country.

1892

William Rainey Harper, founder of the University of Chicago, established the university's press in order to spread his beliefs and philosophy throughout the world.

Q: The University of Chicago press is still in business today. What is its chief distinction?
A: It is the nation's largest university press, as well as the one that has been self-supporting for the longest time.

1893

The publishing firm of Stone & Kimball was formed by two Chicagoans while they were undergraduates at Harvard. Moving their headquarters to Chicago upon graduating, they went on to publish the standard edition of the works of Edgar Allan Poe as well as important works by Robert Louis Stevenson, Henrik Ibsen, and Maurice Maeterlinck before going out of business in 1897.

Q: The firm is also recalled for its publication of *The Chap-Book.* What was it?
A: It was a semimonthly magazine named after small peddlars' books. Witty and irreverent, it featured an avant-garde design that attracted national attention and several imitators.

Q: Publisher Herbert Stuart Stone's father had already made a name for himself in the Chicago literary world. Who was he?
A: Melville Stone was the founding editor of the *Chicago Daily News.*

1893

Finley Peter Dunne began writing in Irish dialect, taking on the persona of a Bridgeport barkeeper and pundit named Martin J. Dooley. Dunne's was the first dialect voice of genius in American literature. He became one of the nation's most widely known columnists after moving to New York in 1900, and Dooley's Bridgeport bar was as well known as Cheers is today.

Trust iv-rybody but cut the cards.
                                        MARTIN J. DOOLEY/FINLEY PETER DUNNE

Q: The parish Dunne grew up in centered around a church that not only survived the Chicago fire but still stands today. It is where all the Irish polls go to mass on St. Paddy's Day. What is its name?
A: Old St. Patrick's Church, located on Des Plaines at Adams Street.

1894

A British journalist and reformer named William T. Stead, who had come to the World's Columbian Exposition, published a tract called *If Christ Came to Chicago: A Plea for the Union of All Who Love in the Service of All Who Suffer*. The moral tract, replete with descriptions of the city's vice dens, became an immediate bestseller.

Q: Stead's book spoke of the "White City" and the "Black City." Which cities were these?
A: Stead was struck by the vivid contrast between the Columbian Exposition's idealized "White City"—the nickname attached to the fair—and the "Black City" where Chicagoans actually lived harsh lives.

Q: Critics have suggested that Stead's moral concern for the poor was less compelling to readers than what other, baser interest?
A: Stead's detailed descriptions of Chicago's vice districts, particularly of the Levee, provided titillation to those readers too timid or otherwise not inclined to partake of those pleasures themselves.

1894

German immigrant Theodore Regensteiner worked out the details of a revolutionary color-printing process in an old photo gallery on Wabash Avenue. He went on to build a gigantic publishing empire.

1895

Frances Willard, president of the Women's Christian Temperance Union and a leading suffragette, had a lighter side—she wrote a delightful book about self-assertion called *How I Learned to Ride the Bicycle,* a skill she did not acquire until her fifties.

1898

Edward H. Amet, having invented the first movie projector in 1894, made a movie of two women boxing and showed it at the Waukegan Opera House. He and his partner, George Spoor, grossed $400 in the first six days. Chicago became part of the new movie business.

Q: One of the most successful of the early silent movie studios was located in Chicago. What was its name, who owned it, and who were its top two stars?

A: Essanay Studios took its name from the initials of the founders, George Spoor and G. M. Anderson. Anderson was an actor who achieved movie fame as Bronco Billy. The other top Essanay star—before he left for California—was Charlie Chaplin.

1898

University of Chicago professor Robert Herrick's first novel set in Chicago was published to generally good reviews, though the local press objected to his harsh treatment of Chicago. Called *The Gospel of Freedom,* it was one of many works that explored Herrick's love/hate relationship with the city.

Q: For what is Herrick known among literary historians?

A: Along with Dreiser, Floyd Dell, Upton Sinclair, Frank Norris and many others, Herrick established what became known as the Chicago school of writing.

If they are united at all, it is in their common acknowledgment that the Chicago of their day provided the best example for the realist of the emerging urban and industrial civilization.

BIOGRAPHER BLAKE NOVENAS IN *ROBERT HERRICK: THE DEVELOPMENT OF A NOVELIST*

1900

L. Frank Baum, who'd lived and worked in places as varied as Syracuse, New York, and Aberdeen, South Dakota, wrote *The Wonderful Wizard of Oz,* but couldn't find a publisher for it. A small Chicago house finally agreed to take it on, but only if Baum and illustrator William Wallace Denslow agreed to cover all the printing expenses. *The Wizard of Oz* was an immediate sensation, and by 1902 five million copies had been sold. Baum followed it with several other *Oz* books and related commercial ventures. After moving to California in 1909, he formed a company to produce Oz movies.

Q: While creating the Yellow Brick Road's characters, Baum lived along one of the North Side's boulevards. A park and lagoon share the same name. What is it?

A: Baum lived at 1667 Humboldt Boulevard, just across North Avenue from Humboldt Park.

Q: Baum may have lived in Humboldt Park, but the park named after his work is in what neighborhood?

A: Oz Park is in the Lincoln Park neighborhood near Armitage and Clark.

Q: The Emerald City of Oz was purportedly inspired by another, real-life city of fantasy. What was it?

A: The White City of the World's Columbian Exposition.

Q: Who were Schuyler Staunton, Edith Van Dyne, and Laura Bancroft?

A: Three of the pseudonyms Baum used for his adult fiction.

1900

Theodore Dreiser's *Sister Carrie* was published in an edition of only 1,000 copies. It drew unfavorable reviews until its publication in England in 1907. Since then it has been widely regarded as the novel that brought American fiction into the 20th century. Born in Indiana, Dreiser moved back and forth between Chicago and New York, working at a succession of newspaper job, until 1912, when he settled in Chicago to begin what became the Frank Cowperwood trilogy.

Q: On whose life did Dreiser base these books, and what were their titles?

A: Based on the life of public transit tycoon Charles Yerkes, the books were *The Titan* (1912), *The Financier* (1914), and *The Stoic* (published posthumously in 1947).

1902

Samuel Eberly Gross won a plagiarism suit against Frenchman Edmond Rostand in a Chicago court. Gross, a developer responsible for the landmark Alta Terrace neighborhood in Wrigleyville, was also a playwright. He claimed that Rostand's popular *Cyrano de Bergerac* was based on his *The Merchant Prince of Cornville,* which he'd written in the 1870s. Though the judge ruled that the French play was a "clear and unmistakable piracy," Rostand steadfastly protested his innocence.

1902

Muckraking novelist Frank Norris published *The Pit,* the first exposé of life in the Board of Trade floor.

1905

Robert S. Abbott founded the *Chicago Defender,* which quickly became a national voice for black people. Abbott's exhortations about job opportunities in the North helped fuel the great migrations of blacks from the South to cities like Chicago.

1905

Dreiser's most commercially successful book, *An American Tragedy,* was published. It dealt with his favorite themes: money, class, and self-gratification.

Q: A movie based on *An American Tragedy* was released in 1951 and became a popular and critical success, winning six Academy Awards. What was the movie's name, and who were its stars?
A: *A Place in the Sun,* starring Montgomery Clift and Elizabeth Taylor.

1906

Upton Sinclair's exposé of the stockyards, *The Jungle,* was published.

> *Here it is at last! The* Uncle Tom's Cabin *of wage slavery!*
> JACK LONDON, ON THE PUBLICATION OF *THE JUNGLE*

Q: Sinclair hoped that his exposé of conditions in the meatpacking business would drive American workers to revolt against capitalism. What effect did it actually have?
A: Widespread indignation about the filthy conditions in the slaughterhouses led to the establishment of federal food inspection laws.

1906

Carl Laemmle used $2,000 in savings to open the White Front Theater at Ashland and Milwaukee. Within three years he was producing motion pictures—*Hiawatha* was his first. In 1912 he formed Universal Film Manufac-turing Company, and in 1915 he opened his 230-acre studio called Universal City in Hollywood.

Q: What was Laemmle's nickname in the film business?
A: Uncle Carl, because he had 70 relatives on his payroll.

Q: The Chicago & North Western Railroad tracks in Ravenswood appeared in what famous movie serial?
A: *The Perils of Pauline,* starring Pearl White as the damsel in distress.

Q: What other North Shore location appeared in many early westerns?
A: Illinois Beach State Park north of Waukegan.

1907

The Cliff Dwellers Club was established, its members being distinguished for their contributions to the arts. Until 1996, its quarters were atop Orchestra Hall.

Q: The Cliff Dwellers Club is thought to have taken its name from a book by one of Chicago's first novelists. What was the book, and who wrote it?
A: *The Cliff Dwellers,* by Henry Blake Fuller, depicted the daily labors of 4,000 people in a building called the Clifton, which Fuller modeled after the Chicago skyscrapers built in the 1890s.

This town of ours labors under one peculiar disadvantage; it is the only great city in the world to which all its citizens have come for the one common, avowed object of making money. There you have its genesis, its growth, its end and object; and there are very few of us who are not attending to that object very strictly.

HENRY BLAKE FULLER

1909

Scott, Foresman & Company began to produce school readers. Later, it published some of the nation's most widely used basic textbooks, including the *Dick and Jane* readers, through which most baby boomers learned to read.

1912

Harriet Monroe founded *Poetry* magazine, which is still published today. Through a friendship with Ezra Pound she attracted work from many major poets, including St. Louis native T .S. Eliot, whose "The Love Song of J. Alfred Prufrock" first appeared in Monroe's publication.

Q: *Poetry* magazine got established when Monroe used her social connections—among other things, her sister was John Wellborn Root's widow—to get several prominent Chicagoans to pledge money for five years toward the new publication. Name some of her investors.
A: Daniel H. Burnham, Samuel Insull, Edith Rockefeller McCormick, Rev. F. W. Gunsaulus, Howard Van Doren Shaw, and Clarence Darrow.

Q: Name some of the poets whom Monroe first published in *Poetry.*

A: Among the many were Richard Aldington, T. S. Eliot, Ford Madox Ford, Robert Frost, James Joyce, D. H. Lawrence, Vachel Lindsay, Edna St. Vincent Millay, Carl Sandburg, Wallace Stevens, Sara Teasdale, William Carlos Williams, and W. B. Yeats.

Q: Monroe was herself a poet, but her first book of verse came to an ignominious end. What was the book, and what was its fate?

A: Monroe printed 5,000 copies of her "Columbian Ode," written for the world's fair, but she wound up using most of the copies for firewood.

1913

Ring Lardner began writing a column for the *Chicago Tribune* covering sports, and quickly built a national reputation by writing the way people talk. He turned sports figures into recognizable personalities. In 1919 he moved to New York and continued to turn out novels while collaborating on plays with George M. Cohan and George S. Kaufman.

Q: What was the name of Lardner's column and who writes it today?

A: "In the Wake of the News," is written nowadays by Bernie Linicome.

Lardner made a literary style out of bad English.
A JEALOUS CONTEMPORARY

Q: Lardner was the model for a character in an F. Scott Fitzgerald novel. Name the character and the book.

A: Abe North in *Tender Is the Night.*

1913

Poet Vachel Lindsay, unhappy in medical school, moved to Chicago to study at the Art Institute. When his poem "General William Booth Enters into Heaven," was published, a critic hailed it as "perhaps the most remarkable poem of a decade."

Q: What vocation did Lindsay wish to pursue before he discovered his talent for writing?

A: Lindsay wanted to become an illustrator or cartoonist.

1913

Ben Hecht arrived in Chicago, got a job on a newspaper, and soon demonstrated a genius for "stealing pictures," a popular journalistic practice of procuring photographs of newsworthy people. When people were subject to unwelcome newspaper coverage, pictures to accompany these tales were highly prized, as was a reporter who could procure them.

Q: Young Ben Hecht became the best picture thief in the business by employing all but which of the following means?

1. Using fire escapes.
2. Crawling through open windows.
3. Posing as a mail carrier.
4. Posing as a gas meter inspector.
5. Breaking into locked houses.

A: All but number 3, which was a federal offense and so was beyond even Hecht's audacious spirit.

Q: A year or so later, the talented Hecht decided to become a playwright, and he collaborated with another aspiring dramatist after whom a theater located on Columbus Drive is named. What's the name of the theater, and who is it named after?
A: The Goodman Theater was built as a memorial to Kenneth Sawyer Goodman, the son of a lumber millionaire. He died shortly after working with Hecht, and his father had the theater built in his memory.

1914

Hecht joined the *Chicago Daily News* and found his talents well employed by legendary editor Henry Justin Smith. He departed the paper briefly around 1920, then rejoined it a year later to produce a daily column.

Q: In 1922 Hecht's columns were collected into a book. What was its title?
A: *1001 Afternoons in Chicago,* published in Chicago by Covici & McGee.

> *[He] loved our paper with an interest that ignored circulation and saw it as a daily novel written by a wild but willing bunch of Balzacs.*
> BEN HECHT ON HENRY JUSTIN SMITH

Q: Among Hecht's many endeavors was the short-lived *Chicago Literary Times,* which irreverently ridiculed politicians, poseurs, and other pompous types. When was it published, and who was his coeditor?
A: Hecht's collaborator was Maxwell Bodenheim, and he brought the paper out from 1923 to 1924.

1914

Robert McCormick inherited control of the *Chicago Tribune*. His eccentric beliefs, coupled with his right-wing politics, never interfered with his building the *Tribune* into a major corporate empire.

Q: McCormick liked to call himself "colonel." How did he acquire the title?

A: During the First World War McCormick served briefly with the American Expeditionary Forces, where he attained the rank of colonel. One battle in which he participated took place near a small French town named Cantigny, the name he gave to his estate in west suburban Wheaton.

Q: In 1924 McCormick acquired a radio station and called it WGN. What did the call letters stand for?

A: "World's Greatest Newspaper," the slogan McCormick had adapted for the *Tribune*.

1915

Edgar Lee Masters's *Spoon River Anthology* was published, and it soon became the most widely read book of poetry in the country. A Kansas native, Masters attended Knox College and became a lawyer. A few years after the publication of *Spoon River Anthology*, he moved to New York, but his subsequent works never attracted much attention, and he died in poverty at the age of 80.

Q: Masters's law partner began acquiring his reputation when defending Eugene Debs after the Pullman Strike. Later he would defend murderers Nathan Leopold and Richard Loeb and a Tennessee schoolteacher named John Scopes. What was his name?

A: Clarence Darrow.

Q: What did Darrow and Masters share besides a law office?

A: A literary bent. Darrow was himself the author of two novels, the more famous being *An Eye for an Eye* (1902).

Q: Masters's one other book that attracted attention was a biography of a gifted poet from Springfield, the author of, among other poems, "Abraham Lincoln Walks at Midnight." What was the name of the book and the poet?

A: Vachel Lindsay's *A Poet in America* was published in 1935 and received the Mark Twain Medal.

1916

"Chicago" by Carl Sandburg—the most famous paen to the Windy City ever penned—was published.

Q: Carl Sandburg may have failed to pass West Point's entrance exam, but he was awarded the Pulitzer Prize in 1940 for his six-volume biography of which commander in chief?
A: Abraham Lincoln.

Q: Often called one of America's natural resources, Sandburg was compared to which other American icon?
A: Mark Twain.

1919

Gasoline Alley, the longest running comic strip in American history, began. It is still running.

1919

On June 9, the *Chicago Tribune* scooped the world by publishing a leaked version of the Treaty of Versailles.

1921

Lee De Forest walked into Western Electric Company in Cicero with a vacuum tube. A quarter of a century later, Chicago had become the world's largest manufacturer of television sets and radios.

1921

Henry Windsor, a young editor fascinated by technology, started a magazine for fellow do-it-yourselfers and called it *Popular Mechanics.* It is still published today.

1921

Chicago native Edgar Rice Burroughs, before he became famous as the creator of Tarzan, wrote *The Mucker* about a Chicago gangster who is sentenced to life in prison for a murder he didn't commit, but who is saved by a timely last-minute confession and lives happily ever after.

Q: Who published the first Tarzan book, and why?
A: A. C. McClurg published it only after Burroughs hounded him incessantly.

Q: Burroughs grew up in a suburb associated with another famous writer. What town was it, and who was the other writer?

A: Ernest Hemingway also grew up in Oak Park.

Q: What other Chicagoan became famous from Burroughs's most famous creation?

A: Johnny Weismuller grew up in Chicago and went on to become the most popular movie *Tarzan*.

1921

On November 11 the first Chicago radio station began to broadcast. Its call letters were KYW, and it has since been moved to Philadelphia.

1922

Two radio stations destined to play large roles in Chicago opened for business—WGN and WMAQ (then called WGU).

1923

The printing and publishing industry employed a total of 35,062 people in Chicago.

1924

Dr. Morris Fishbein assumed the editorship of the *Journal of the American Medical Association,* a post he held until the 1950s. He was also the first medical editor of *Time* magazine. Throughout his long career, he attacked quackery, promoted sound medical practices, and was generally regarded as the most influential person in American medicine during his time.

1924

Edna Ferber, who had arrived in Chicago in 1910 as a 23-year-old reporter and short-story writer, was the first Jewish writer to win a Pulitzer Prize.

Q: For what book did Ferber win her Pulitzer? Where was it set?

A: *So Big* was set in South Holland and Chicago.

Q: Chicago figured large in Ferber's first novel as well. What was it called, and when was it published?

A: *Fanny Herself,* about a young woman who worked in a Chicago mail-order firm, was published in 1917.

Q: In addition to Chicago, Ferber immortalized many other landmarks of American geography. Name five of them and the books that glorified them.

A: The Mississippi River *(Showboat,* 1926), Oklahoma *(Cimarron,* 1930), Wisconsin and Michigan *(Come and Get It,* 1935), Texas *(Giant,* 1952), and Alaska *(Ice Palace,* 1958).

I've written a lot about Chicago, really, but I'm practically never thought of as having written anything about Chicago. Strange.
EDNA FERBER, AFTER SHE HAD SETTLED IN NEW YORK

Q: Twenty-five years later, another Chicago female writer made another historic first vis-à-vis the Pulitzer Prize. Who was she, and what had she done?

A: Gwendolyn Brooks, the first black writer to win a Pulitzer, won it for her collection of poems, *Annie Allen.*

Q: Which African-American pair of artist brothers flourished in the 1930s, albeit dealing with different subject matters in different media?

A: Archibald J. Motley Jr. was a painter whose candid depictions aimed at portraying African-American life as accurately as possible; his brother, Willard Motley, was a novelist who wrote mostly about ethnic whites.

Live fast, die young, and make a good-looking corpse.
WILLARD MOTLEY, IN HIS NOVEL *KNOCK ON ANY DOOR* (1947)

Q: Who starred in *Fibber McGee and Molly?*
A: Jim Jordan and Marian Jordan.

1924

WLS, named for its owner Sears, Roebuck (World's Largest Store) was sold to *Prairie Farmer,* which instituted the WLS *Barn Dance,* a Saturday variety show that ran for nearly four decades.

Q: A famous comedian and an equally famous cowboy got their starts on *Barn Dance.* Name them.
A: George Gobel and Gene Autry.

1926

WCFL, owned by the Chicago Federation of Labor, began operation.

1927

WIND (the IND stands for Indiana) began broadcasting.

1927

There were 1,572 printing and publishing plants in Chicago, employing 33,176 people.

1927

Sears Roebuck & Company brought the *Encyclopaedia Britannica* to Chicago by underwriting most of the $2.5 million cost of the 14th edition of the encyclopedia. The edition contained 38 million words and included the work of 3,500 contributors. Sears gave the publication to the University of Chicago in the 1940s.

Q: What publishing record does the *Encyclopaedia Britannica* hold?
A: It is the oldest continuously published reference work in the English language.

1928

Hecht and Charles MacArthur collaborated on the classic play *The Front Page.*

Q: *The Front Page* has been made into a film four different times. Name the films and the years in which they were made.
A: *The Front Page* (1931), *His Girl Friday* (1940), *The Front Page* (1974), and *Switching Channels* (1988).

Q: Hecht's partner Charles MacArthur was married to a famous actress. Their son became a famous actor. Name both of them.
A: Helen Hayes and James MacArthur.

Q: Walter Burns, the cantankerous editor in *The Front Page,* was based on a real-life Chicago newspaperman. What was his name, and what paper did he work for?
A: Walter Howey of the *Tribune* (not the *Daily News*!).

Q: Before there was Riccardo's and the Billy Goat Tavern, there was a hangout on Wells Street that attracted *Daily News* reporters and a host of other literary types. What was it called, and who were some others who frequented it?
A: Schlogls, and it was especially popular with Margaret Anderson, Sherwood Anderson, Ring Lardner, and Carl Sandburg.

1928

On March 19 Freeman Gosden and Charles Correll began the *Amos 'n Andy* show. Although the show depicted urban blacks with broad Jim Crow strokes, Gosden and Correll themselves were white.

Q: What radio show did Gosden and Correll do before *Amos 'n Andy?*
A: *Sam 'n Henry,* which covered the same general theme.

1929

WGN was the first broadcaster to install police radios in the officers' cars. Soon police radio was adopted in every city of the land, and Chicago-based Motorola became famous for its auto radio receivers.

1929

Jack L. Cooper became the country's first African-American radio personality when his live 60-minute variety show, *The All-Negro Hour,* premiered on WSBC radio in Chicago.

Q: What else was Cooper famous for doing on radio?
A: Since baseball was not yet integrated, Cooper broadcast scores from the old Negro leagues. He also broadcast the Bud Billken Day Parade, a major event in the black community each August.

1930

The comic strip *Blondie* was first introduced in a Chicago newspaper.

1930

While helping William H. Elson, superintendent of schools in Cleveland, revise his reading textbooks, Dr. William S. Gray of the University of Chicago introduced a system in which the number of new words introduced on a page in a primer was controlled.

1931

Fibber McGee and Molly began on Chicago station WENR as part of the show *Smackout* before going national on NBC in 1935.

1931

Dick Tracy, the comic strip, was created for the *Chicago Tribune* by Chester Gould.

1931

On April 7 the radio show of *Little Orphan Annie* went on the air, following the success of the comic strip. It ran until 1940.

1932

George Dillon's *The Flowering Stone* became the first book of Chicago verse to win a Pulitzer Prize.

1932

James T. Farrell published *Young Lonigan, A Boyhood in the Streets* at the age of 28. Like his most famous character, Studs Lonigan, Farrell grew up in the South Side Washington Park neighborhood, still an Irish enclave in the 1930s.

Q: Name the other books in the Studs Lonigan trilogy.
A: *The Young Manhood of Studs Lonigan* and *Judgment Day*.

Q: What was Farrell's college ambition?
A: To publish 25 novels. And he did.

Q: A popular Chicago figure one decade younger than Lonigan took his nickname from Farrell's character. Who is he, and what does he do?
A: Studs Terkel is a radio interviewer and Pulitzer Prize-winning author.

1933

In August the first issue of a new magazine appeared, the brainchild of legendary editor Arnold Gingrich—*Esquire* was aimed solely at sophisticated men.

Q: In what building were the *Esquire* offices? What famous magazine was also published in that building?
A: The Palmolive Building, Michigan Avenue and Walton Street. Sixty years later, Hugh Hefner bought the building, moved *Playboy's* offices there, and changed the name of the entire building to match.

Q: What future magazine editor got his start working at *Esquire?*
A: Hugh Hefner. Who else?

1936

Colonel Frank Knox, the publisher of the *Daily News,* left the newsroom to run for vice president on the Republican ticket behind Alf Landon. They carried only two states.

Q: Roosevelt bore no grudges. To what position did he later appoint Knox?
A: Secretary of the navy.

You tell the boys to sit back on their seats, take their hats off, and make a better newspaper than ever. And while you are about it, take your own hat off.
COLONEL FRANK KNOX, ON HIS ARRIVAL AT THE *DAILY NEWS*

1936

The popular *Alice and Jerry* readers, published by Row Peterson and Company, were the first textbooks to be published in full-color offset.

1937

One-third of all radios produced in the United States were made in Chicago.

Q: Eight Chicago companies produced radios for RCA under license. Name them.
A: Grigsby-Grunow, All-American Mohawk, Howard Radio, Bremer-Tully, Electrical Research Laboratories, Fansteel Products, U.S. Radio, and Zenith Radio.

1938

In Old Chicago, starring Tyrone Power, Alice Faye, Don Ameche, and Alice Brady, told the highly fictionalized story of the O'Leary family, climaxing in the Chicago Fire of 1871. The movie was directed by Henry King, and Alice Brady won an Academy Award for best supporting actress.

1940

Novelist Richard Wright published *Native Son,* the first novel by a black writer to be chosen as a Book-of-the-Month-Club selection.

Q: Where did *Native Son* take place, who was its main character, and what happened to him?
A: Chicago's South Side. Bigger Thomas is a black man who, in Wright's words, was "whipped before he was born." He accidentally kills a wealthy white girl and is sentenced to death.

Q: Where did Wright die?
A: Paris, France, where he lived the last 13 years of his life.

There is more freedom in one square block of Paris than in all of the United States.
RICHARD WRIGHT

Q: *Native Son* was not the first novel about black life in Chicago. In 1930 another very famous black writer published an autobiographical novel set partly in Chicago. What was the book, and who wrote it?
A: *Not Without Laughter* by Langston Hughes.

1941

Timing is everything. Marshall Field III debuted a new Chicago newspaper, the *Chicago Sun,* on a great news day—December 7, Pearl Harbor Day.

1943

"Kup's Column," by legendary Chicago newspaper columnist Irv Kupcinet, first appeared on January 18.

1943

Television station WBKB, later to become the station we know today as WLS, began broadcasting in Chicago.

Q: In 1945 a radio announcer who later went on to nationwide fame as a talk show personality began hosting the *1160 Club,* a midnight radio show on WNBQ-Radio. Name him.
A: Dave Garroway.

1944

A first novel by Saul Bellow, destined to become Chicago's most famous late twentieth-century writer, was published.

Q: What was the name of the novel?
A: *Dangling Man.*

Q: For four years, between 1938 and 1942, Bellow wrote for what famous organization?
A: The W.P.A. (Works Progress Administration).

Q: Although identified with the University of Chicago, Bellow taught at another Chicago college first. Name it.
A: The Pestalozzi-Froebel Teachers College.

1945

Ebony magazine began publication in November. Along with its sister publication *Jet,* it made Johnson Publishing Company the largest publisher of magazines for the African-American community. In 1996 *Ebony's* circulation was 1,800,000.

1946

WBBM-TV started broadcasting on Channel Four. A decade later, it moved to its present position on Channel Two.

Q: In 1947 a television mystery show had the conclusion to each week's puzzle published the next day in a Chicago newspaper. Name the show and the paper.
A: *Chicagoland Mystery Players.* The *Chicago Tribune* published the mystery's outcome, but the *Tribune's* connection dried up when the show went national.

1949

Chicago Deadline, starring Alan Ladd, Arthur Kennedy, Donna Reed, and directed by Lewis Allen, was released but Hollywood's cameras didn't come within 2,000 miles of Chicago during its filming.

Q: It was later remade into a TV series, also starring Alan Ladd. What was it called?
A: *Fame Is the Name of the Game.*

1949

A TV variety show where guests dropped by regularly to chat and sing was hosted by University of Chicago-trained lawyer turned interviewer, Studs Terkel.

Q: What was the name of the show, and who was the featured musician?
A: It was called, simply enough, *Studs' Place.* The musician was Chicago folksinger and songwriter Win Stracke.

Q: *Stand By for Crime* was a one-season show where viewers called in to guess who committed the weekly crime. It gave an important career boost to a young journalist. Name him.
A: Mike Wallace.

1949

WMAQ-TV, then known as WNBQ, began broadcasting from the Merchandise Mart. The NBC-affiliate would remain in its Mart studios into the 1980s, when it moved to the NBC Plaza building.

1949

Lauren Bacall and Humphrey Bogart honeymooned at the Ambassador East Hotel, augmenting the hotel's—and its famed Pump Room's—reputation as the place for visiting celebrities to stay.

1950s

Before New York (and later Hollywood) dominated television, Chicago produced a number of TV shows that achieved national popularity, among them *Kukla, Fran and Ollie, Mr. Wizard, Super Circus,* and *The Zoo Parade.*

Q: What was the original name of the *Kukla, Fran and Ollie Show?*
A: *Junior Jamboree.*

Q: A Northwestern University professor became a Sunday afternoon fixture on national TV in the late 1950s. Name the professor and the show.
A: Linguist Dr. Bergen Evans hosted *Down You Go.*

1951

Nelson Algren won the first National Book Award for Fiction for *The Man with the Golden Arm.*

Q: An earlier Algren novel had the honor of being banned from the Chicago Public Library. What was it, and what group disliked it?
A: *Never Come Morning* (1945), an indictment of life in Chicago's Polish-American slums, was banned at the behest of the Polish Roman Catholic Union.

Q: Along with Richard Wright, Algren was a long-time member of what leftist literary club?
A: The Chicago John Reed Club, named after the author of *Ten Days That Shook the World* about the 1917 Russian revolution.

Q: Algren carried on a long-term love affair with a French writer who was almost—but not quite—married to another famous French writer who won—but did not accept—the Nobel Prize for literature. Name them.
A: Simone de Beauvoir and Jean-Paul Sartre.

Never play cards with a guy named Doc, never eat at a place called Mom's, and never sleep with someone whose problems are greater than your own.
NELSON ALGREN

1951

The next year, Algren published *City On the Make,* which many critics consider the most perceptive commentary ever written about Chicago.

Q: In the same year, another famous commentary on Chicago appeared. Who wrote it, and how did it find its way into the city's consciousness?

A: A. J. Liebling published a series of articles in *The New Yorker* that lambasted Chicago's insularity and humorlessness. When he dubbed Chicago the "Second City," Liebling unwittingly laid the groundwork for the theatrical troupe that became Chicago's most famous contribution to American humor.

1952

Chicago Calling, starring Dan Duryea and Mary Anderson, came out.

1953

The first issue of *Playboy* magazine appeared in November.

Q: What was the original name of *Playboy,* which Hefner dropped at the last minute?

A: *Stag Party.*

> *I don't need to leave. Why should I? I've got more right here now inside this house than most people ever find in a lifetime!*
> HUGH HEFNER, ASKED WHY HE HAD LEFT HIS NEAR
> NORTH MANSION ONLY NINE TIMES IN THREE YEARS

> *The sweetest, most selfish man I've ever known.*
> CHICAGO RESTAURATEUR ARNIE MORTON, WHOM
> HEFNER HIRED TO RUN THE FIRST PLAYBOY CLUB

1953

Mail-order houses with their catalogs contributed significantly to the printing business in Chicago. Sears had more than 50 million copies of their catalogs printed by R. R. Donnelley and the Reuben Donnelley Company printed 3,700,000 phone directories for the Chicago area as well as supplying such directories to other cities in the nation.

1954

The most widely circulated magazines in the nation—*Life, Look, Ebony, Jet, Popular Mechanics*—were printed by R. R. Donnelley, along with a major portion of the almost 2,000 trade magazines published in the United States.

1955

Colonel Robert McCormick, the relentlessly conservative publisher of the *Chicago Tribune,* died, and reporters there were once again free to use the word *Democrat.*

1955

Chicago Syndicate, with Dennis O'Keefe, Abbe Lane, and Paul Stewart, arrived at theaters to no particular acclaim.

1956

Ex-*Daily News* reporter Meyer Levin published *Compulsion,* the story of the Leopold-Loeb murder case and was later sued by Leopold for "invasion of privacy." Leopold lost.

Q: What famous journal did Levin uncover while on assignment in Europe and translate into English?
A: *The Diary of Anne Frank.* He later wrote a stage version that was the subject of a bitter lawsuit between Levin and Otto Frank, Anne's father.

Q: In 1940 Levin published a novel based on a famous Chicago labor incident. What was it?
A: *Citizens* was based on the 1937 conflict at Republic Steel.

1956

Ikuko Toguri d'Aquino settled in Chicago in 1956 after going through the longest treason trial in U.S. history for her role as a Japanese radio broadcaster.

Q: What was d'Aquino's radio name?
A: Tokyo Rose.

1956

WNBQ, part of the NBC network owned by David Sarnoff's RCA Corporation, the pioneer in color television, became the first TV station in America to transmit all of its live programs in color.

Q: In 1957 a semi-gritty television show set in Chicago called M-Squad starred a tough-guy newcomer who later won an Academy Award for best actor. Who was the actor, and what was the name of his character?
A: Lee Marvin played Lieutenant Frank Ballinger.

Q: Name the 1957 movie directed by Sidney Salkow and starring Brian Keith and Beverly Garland that dealt with gangsters in Chicago.
A: *Chicago Confidential.*

1959

Marshall Field IV bought the *Chicago Daily News.*

1959

Lion at My Heart, the first novel by Harry Mark Petrakis, was published, the first in his stream of books and stories about Greek-American life in Chicago.

1959

The Untouchables, one of the most successful—and controversial—television series ever, premiered. While the show was wildly popular for four seasons, its violence spawned viewer protest and even a defamation lawsuit from the Al Capone estate.

Q: The success of *The Untouchables* led to a full-length movie nearly 30 years later which, unlike the TV series, was actually filmed in Chicago. Who wrote and who directed the 1987 version?
A: Brian DePalma directed it from a script by David Mamet.

Q: Five different actors have played Al Capone in films. Name them.
A: Edward G. Robinson, Rod Steiger, Jason Robards Jr., Neville Brand, and George Raft.

1967

Don Lee, a black poet recently arrived from Detroit, started publishing poems and eventually formed Third World Press, the largest African-American publisher in the country.

Q: What did Don Lee do after forming Third World Press?
A: He changed his name to Haki Madhubuti and became one of Chicago's most prolific writers.

1968

The Young Runaways starring Brooke Bundy purported to depict the hippie scene in Chicago. It died fast.

1971

The Chicago Teddy Bears, a sitcom starring Dean Jones and Jamie Farr of *M*A*S*H* fame, died after one season.

1972

One of the most successful, and most flattering to Chicago, of all TV shows set in Chicago, began a six-year run—*The Bob Newhart Show.*

Q: What town did the TV visuals show Bob Newhart passing through on the way from his 5500 North Lake Shore Drive apartment on his way to the Loop?
A: Wilmette. So much for geography.

Q: One of the pioneer sitcoms centered around a black family became immensely popular during the 1974 television season. Set in Cabrini-Green, it was produced by veteran producer Norman Lear. Name it.
A: *Good Times.*

1972

Duck Variations by David Mamet was the first in a series of plays by the Chicago playwright to be produced in Chicago and later New York.

1974

On September 13 *Chicago Today* newspaper suspended publication, the first of the city's "big four" newspapers to go under.

1976

The *McLean Stevenson Show* about the owner of an Evanston hardware store died in its first season on TV.

1978

On March 4 *The Chicago Daily News* suspended publication after 100 years. It is still regarded as having published the best writing of any Chicago paper.

1979

Television often creates new movie stars. The 1979 comedy *Working Stiffs* died in its first season, but it introduced two then unknown actors as janitors in a Chicago office building—Jim Belushi and Michael Keaton.

1981

American Dream, a sitcom about a couple that moved from Park Ridge to the city for wacky urban adventures, lasted one season.

1981

The TV series that finally put Chicago on the map, *Hill Street Blues,* began its pioneering seven-year run. Set in Chicago (though filmed in Hollywood), *Blues* was one of the most widely acclaimed police dramas in TV history.

Q: What actor played the captain of the Hill Street precinct, and what was his character's name?
A: Daniel J. Travanti played Captain Frank Furillo.

1982

In a possible attempt to emulate the success of *Hill Street Blues, Chicago Story* was a three-in-one show about cops, lawyers, and doctors. It died early, possibly because of its 90-minute length.

1983

Webster, with Alex Karras playing a football player turned sportscaster, ran for six years. Its connection to Chicago was limited to the scriptwriter's fantasy.

1984

E/R, an innovative series about a Chicago hospital, has more than a tangential connection with Chicago. It was based on a play produced at the Organic Theater. Alas, audiences cared little, and it only lasted one season.

1984

Veteran journalist John Callaway launched *Chicago Tonight,* a four-times-a-week discussion show on WTTW, which has become the longest-running daily local show in American television history.

Q: How is John Callaway referred to by people across the country who have appeared on his show?
A: "That fat guy in Chicago." Callaway tells the story on himself.

1985

Once again, the pull of *Hill Street Blues* did not rub off when *Lady Blue,* about a tough lady cop, died after one season.

1985

Mary Tyler Moore was supposed to have been magic, but her show *Mary,* about a Chicago-based tabloid columnist, lasted only one season.

Q: Name the real ex-cop from Chicago who played a cop on *Crime Story,* a series that was actually filmed in Chicago beginning in 1986.
A: Dennis Farina.

Q: Name the 1986 TV series about a Mediterranean shepherd who immigrated to Chicago and moves in with his cousin. How long did it last on TV?
A: *Perfect Stranger.* It ran for six seasons.

1986

On June 30 Australian media-magnate Rupert Murdoch bought the *Chicago Sun-Times.* Veteran columnist Mike Royko, himself an import from the old *Daily News,* promptly departed for the *Tribune.*

> *The only thing I've changed since I crossed the street was my socks.*
> MIKE ROYKO, UPON CROSSING MICHIGAN AVENUE
> FROM THE *SUN-TIMES* TO THE *TRIBUNE*

1987

Sable, a TV series about a Chicago children's-book-writer-turned-crime-fighter, lasted one season.

1987

Chicago lawyer Scott Turow published *Presumed Innocent,* which became not only a bestseller and a movie, but revived the genre of courtroom thriller.

1989

Anything But Love, about journalism at the fictitious *Chicago Weekly* magazine, was a moderate success in that it managed to run for three seasons.

Q: Name the female star of *Anything But Love,* and name her equally famous parents.
A: Jamie Lee Curtis is the daughter of Janet Leigh and Tony Curtis.

1990

The original *Uncle Buck* movie, starring the late John Candy, was filmed on location in Evanston and was a big hit. The TV series, filmed in Hollywood, died in its first season.

Q: Which of these other movies were also shot in Chicago?

1. *Looking for Mr. Goodbar.*
2. *The Blues Brothers.*
3. *Ordinary People.*
4. *Rich and Famous.*
5. *The Fury.*

A: All of them.

1992

Angel Street, about a rookie lady cop a.k.a. "The Hill Street Blues Lady Story," died in its first season, despite the presence of Robin Givens.

Q: Name the 1994 series about a Canadian Mountie who came to Chicago to work the streets as a cop.
A: *Due South.*

1995

In November *Chicago Books in Review* published its inaugural issue. It was the first independent literary periorical to be published in Chicago since the demise in 1924 of *Chicago Literary Times.*

CHAPTER 7

Athens on the Prairie

Remember that our sons and grandsons are going to do things that would stagger us. Let your watchword be order, and your beacon, beauty.

DANIEL H. BURNHAM, CA. 1912

Build the city up, tear the city down.
Come, let us found a city.

CARL SANDBURG

Painters may flock to Paris, playwrights to New York, actors to Los Angeles, but the one place where every architect in the world dreams of testing his mettle is in Chicago. The Windy City remains the acknowledged world leader in architecture. As with so much else about Chicago, its architecture is a mixture of commerce and art.

"Form ever follows function," Louis Sullivan wrote in the late 1880s, and what Sullivan, his contemporaries, and heirs accomplished may well be regarded centuries from now the same way we regard Athens in the age of Pericles. But we must also note that Sullivan died in poverty 30 years after his daringly innovative Transportation Building was overshadowed by the neo-classicism that prevailed at the World's Columbian Exposition—he couldn't get any commissions. Sullivan's student, Frank Lloyd Wright, left town in disgust when the new century was only a decade old. Chicago was too busy making money to notice the wonders it had wrought.

It was not until the 1970s, when a group of architects got together to spoof the Tribune Tower competition of 1922, that Chicago reclaimed its architectural heritage. In the building boom that followed, architects were suddenly on a par with movie stars and football coaches in the fame department.

It had all begun 150 years earlier when a New Hampshire jack-of-all-trades named George Washington Shaw built a warehouse on the river's banks, with nothing but nails and two-by-fours. The following year, a carpenter from Connecticut named Augustine Taylor systematized Shaw's method in constructing St. Mary's Church, and the balloon-frame building was born. Chicago had found a way to shelter itself, and it has gone on innovating ever since.

1833

St. Mary's was established as the first Catholic parish in town, and its church became the city's first balloon-frame building. This method of construction was made necessary by a shortage of wood and labor. It enabled Chicago not only to grow up quickly but to burn down fast. Nonetheless, it revolutionized the construction of wood-framed buildings.

Q: What is balloon-frame construction?
A: Simply, it is lumber nailed together into a frame that shapes and supports a building. It eliminated the necessity of mortised joints at the same time that it replaced heavy posts and beams with inexpensive milled lumber. Virtually all houses in America today are built with balloon frames.

1837

Henry B. Clarke built a substantial country house on his farm south of the city, not far from where the Fort Dearborn settlers were massacred. It is the oldest building still standing in Chicago and is open to the public as part of the Prairie Avenue Historic District.

1837

Mayor William Ogden brought his friend John Van Osdel to Chicago to design a house for him on Chicago's North Side. Osdel stayed to become Chicago's first architect.

1847

The city of Chicago declared the land along the lakefront south to 11th Street public property and named the area Lake Park. The west side of Michigan Avenue became the city's first fashionable residential street.

A grant of 20 acres of the Military Reservation [Fort Dearborn] shall be reserved in all time to come for a public square.
A RESOLUTION OF THE TOWN COUNCIL IN 1833, REFERRING TO THE LAND
EAST OF MICHIGAN AVENUE BETWEEN MADISON AND RANDOLPH

I foresee a time, not very distant, when Chicago will need for its fast increasing population a park or parks in each division. Of these parks I have a vision. They are all improved and connected with a wide avenue ... surrounding the city with a magnificent chain of parks and parkways that have not their equal in the World.

JOHN S. WRIGHT, EDITOR OF THE *PRAIRIE FARMER*, IN 1841

1853

Van Osdel designed the two-story Cook County Courthouse. A third story was added five years later. Its domed tower provided an uninterrupted view of the growing city. Its iron-gated yard was one of the city's first landscaped public areas.

1855

With the city's population already approaching 100,000, sanitation was becoming a big problem. To begin solving it, city engineer Ellis Chesbrough introduced a plan to raise by five to 10 feet the level of city streets.

Q: Though pulling the city from the swamp is the aesthetic reason for raising the street level, a far more practical reason was behind the move. What was it?

A: Chesbrough had to figure out an efficient means of building a new sewage system for the burgeoning city. Installing new drainage pipes on top of the old streets was the most practical means. That meant raising the level of the streets and sidewalks.

Q: Two years later, an energetic young carpenter oversaw the raising of an entire block of buildings on Lake Street between Clark and LaSalle, a block that included the classy Tremont Hotel. What was his name, and how did he do it?

A: He was George Pullman, whose carpentry skills were to become useful a decade later when he redesigned the railway sleeping car. The project took 500 men and 2,500 jackscrews, but not a guest was disturbed nor a window in the hotel broken.

1855

At the urging of William Ogden, a Boston-born portrait painter named George Peter Alexander Healy arrived in Chicago from Paris, where he had established a name for himself. Ogden promised Healy that painting portraits in Chicago would make him rich, and it did. Healy made Chicago his base until he died at age 81, the year his Ontario Street home had served as a gathering place for French artists during the Columbian Exposition.

Q: Healy reportedly painted over 500 Chicagoans during his first dozen years in the city. What happened to the canvases?

A: Almost all of them were destroyed in the Chicago fire. When the Art Institute was established after the fire, he presented it with its first gift, his painting called "The American Fathers."

Q: In lieu of paying the $1,000 due Healy for a portrait, a financially embarrassed Chicago businessman in 1860 offered instead a plot of land near State Street and Chicago Avenue. When Healy went to register the deed, what did the city clerk tell him?

A: "Why that land on the lakefront isn't worth $10."

1856

Although the city had been incorporated for less than 20 years, a Chicago Historical Society was established on April 24.

1867

Chesbrough, still struggling with the city's sanitation problems, laid the cornerstone for the Chicago Water Tower on March 25. Its purpose was to house a 137-foot standpipe, which powered the distribution of fresh lake water through pipes in the city's streets.

Q: A noted English visitor to Chicago who had called the Water Tower a "castellated monstrosity with pepper boxes stuck all over it," said he was impressed with the pumping machinery, describing it as "simple, grand, and natural." Who was the visitor?

A: Oscar Wilde.

The simpering Oscar comes,
The West awaits his wonder.
As bullfrogs list to beating drums,
Or hearken to the thunder....

THE GREETING OFFERED TO WILDE BY THE
DAILY NEWS PRIOR TO HIS ARRIVAL

1869

At the urging of a state health commissioner and with the active support of real estate developers and civic boosters, Chicago established boards to oversee the development of an ambitious ring of parks and boulevards around the city—the plan John Wright had foreseen 20 years earlier.

Q: Some well-known architects and landscape planners designed this system of parks. Who were they?

A: Primarily Chicagoan William LeBaron Jenney, who would further distinguish himself as an architect and who was responsible for the west parks; Frederick Law Olmsted, the landscape architect responsible for New York's Central Park and west suburban Riverside, designed the south parks.

Q: This ring of parks still exists, extending 28 miles from Jackson Park on the south to Lincoln Park on the north, including among others: Washington, Douglas, Garfield, and Humboldt Parks as well as several boulevards. Name some of the latter.

A: King Drive and the Midway Plaisance, Garfield, California and Independence Boulevards on the South Side, Sacramento, Humboldt, and Logan Boulevards on the North Side.

Q: Only one part of the boulevard system was not built as originally conceived. What was it?

A: Commercial and residential construction had proceeded too quickly along Diversey Parkway for it to be widened into a boulevard.

Q: In the same year the park system was organized, the federal government started developing Calumet Harbor. Why was this beneficial for the city's lakefront?

A: Moving the Port of Chicago down to Calumet meant that the downtown lakefront could be saved for recreational purposes.

1869

Field, Leiter and Company opened on State Street, signaling the accomplishment of Potter Palmer's plan to shift the city's axis from east-west along Lake Street to north-south, with State the main commercial thoroughfare.

1871

The Great Chicago Fire destroyed 17,450 buildings on 2.7 square miles of the city and left 90,000 people homeless.

Q: No downtown structure south of the Chicago River survived the fire; only four structures north of it did. What were they?

A: As most anyone who has ever visited Chicago knows, the Water Tower and Pumping Station on Chicago Avenue remained intact after the fire, as did the homes of Mahlon Ogden, brother of the mayor, and police officer Richard Bellinger's cottage at 2121 North Hudson Street. The Ogden home was later razed, and the Newberry Library built on its site. Bellinger's wooden cottage still stands. Like the Water Tower, it was designed by William Boyington.

1873

The first Palmer House Hotel had opened just a few weeks before the fire. In January, 15 months after the fire, a new one opened that featured a barbershop floor studded with silver dollars.

1874

Marshall Field commissioned New York architect Richard Hunt to design a home for him on Prairie Avenue, which was rapidly developing as the street of the city's elite.

1881

Construction began on Pullman, the nation's first planned industrial town. Located 10 miles south of the city on the western shore of Lake Calumet, it was built to house workers at Pullman's Palace Car Company. He felt the clean and pleasant environment would increase his workers' productivity. He also thought the town should turn a profit.

Q: How did Pullman explain using the name Pullman for the new town?
A: He claimed the name was derived from the first half of his name and the second half of the architect's name, Solon S. Beman, thus avoiding charges of immodesty.

1882

When built in 1882 the 10-story Montauk Building was the city's tallest. Some claim for it the distinction of being the world's first skyscraper.

1882

The Chicago Academy of Design changed its name to the Art Institute of Chicago at the urging of its new president, Charles L. Hutchinson.

1882

Potter and Bertha Palmer built their castle on the lakefront north of the river, beginning the shift of fashionable residences up from the South Side. The eccentric house was built without outside doorknobs, so doors had to be opened by servants from within.

Q: The Palmers' legacies to Chicago are numerous and varied. Potter's chief accomplishments were in real estate, Bertha's in art. What collection is she most known for?

A: While in Paris drumming up support for the Columbian Exposition in 1893, she acquired the most extensive collection of French Impressionists on this side of the Atlantic. Many pieces in her collection were loaned to the Palace of Fine Arts at the fair and later given to the Art Institute.

What is art? In my limited conception, it is the work of some genius graced with extraordinary proclivities not given to ordinary mortals. Speaking of art, my husband can spit over a freight car.

BERTHA HONORE PALMER

1885

Construction was completed on William LeBaron Jenney's Home Insurance Building, the world's first building to be hung on a metal frame or skeleton.

Q: What was the importance of skeletal construction?

A: Before architects like Jenney figured out how to do steel-framed skeletal construction, buildings had to be held up by load-bearing walls.

Q: Doesn't Chicago have a distinction in that category, too?

A: Yes. The 1889 Monadnock Building is still the world's tallest building with load-bearing walls. Its walls, which hold up its 16 stories—-are six to eight feet thick at the base.

Q: Jenney was also a mentor for many Chicago architects. Who of the following never worked in his office?

1. Daniel Burnham
2. William Holabird
3. John Von Osdel
4. Martin Roche
5. Howard Van Doren Shaw
6. Louis Sullivan
7. Frank Lloyd Wright.

A: Von Osdel and Wright. Von Osdel, generally considered Chicago's first architect, was in practice far earlier than Jenney, who didn't even begin his firm until the late 1860s. Wright didn't start his practice until after most of Jenney's significant work had been done.

A new spirit of beauty is being developed and perfected, and even now its first achievements are beginning to delight us. This is not old things made over; it is new. It springs out of the past, but it is not tied to it; it studies the traditions, but it is not enslaved by them.

JOHN WELLBORN ROOT

1885

Burnham and Root's glorious Rookery Building, with its spiral staircase and sparkling white light court, opened at LaSalle and Adams.

Q: Why is that building called the Rookery?
A: It was once the site of Chicago's city hall, and a garage at its rear attracted birds; hence, the name.

Q: Four other noted Chicago architects have worked on the Rookery's lobby. Who are they, and when did they work on it?
A: In 1907 Frank Lloyd Wright renovated it; in 1931 it was redone by William Drummond. In 1992 the McClier Corporation restored it to Wright's plan under the direction of architect William Hasbrouck.

1889

Adler and Sullivan's remarkable Auditorium Building was completed. Built at the request of culture buff and developer Ferdinand Peck, it was based on the idea that its commercial spaces—a hotel and office tower—would subsidize its 4,300-seat theater. Other distinctions include perfect sight lines from even the most inexpensive seat in the theater and magically good acoustics. The building was considered so extraordinary that both President Benjamin Harrison and Vice President Levi Morton showed up for its opening.

1889

The "suburban" villages of Hyde Park, Kenwood, and others were incorporated into Chicago, adding substantially to its area and population. Real estate developer Paul Cornell had begun building up the area 40 years earlier by acquiring land and persuading the Illinois Central to stop there.

Q: Raised downstate and trained as a lawyer, Cornell had a mishap on his first night in Chicago. What was it?

A: His hotel room was broken into and all his savings were stolen. He recovered quickly, however, getting a job as a lawyer.

Q: As a member of the South Park Commission, Cornell was responsible for bringing what noted landscape architect to town?
A: He hired Frederick Law Olmsted to design Jackson and Washington Parks, plus the Midway Plaisance to connect them.

1892

The 21-story Masonic Temple Building designed by Burnham and Root became the world's tallest when built in 1892 at the corner of State and Randolph Streets.

Q: The construction of tall buildings on Chicago's spongy soil was made possible by what innovation?
A: The floating foundation provided a way of anchoring buildings when bedrock was too far down to anchor buildings in the customary fashion. It used concrete rafts that distributed the building's weight sufficiently to keep it afloat in soft soil.

Q: What happened to the Masonic Temple Building? (There is now a Walgreen's on the corner it once dominated.)
A: In 1931 both the Masonic Temple and Henry Hobson Richardson's monumental Marshall Field wholesale annex on Adams Street between Wells and Franklin were demolished so taxes wouldn't have to be paid on them.

1893

In the first public use of electric lighting the World's Columbian Exposition was illuminated by 7,000 arc and 120,000 incandescent lamps. Its classically inspired Court of Honor would influence public buildings for the next three decades.

Q: Architect Louis Sullivan, whose colorful Transportation Building was an exception to the fair's dominant building type, made an uncomplimentary comment about the fair's architecture. What was it?
A: Sullivan said it would set American architecture back 25 years, and he was right. Not until Art Deco and Art Modern became popular in the 1920s did classicism lose its chic.

1896

The two bronze lions that stand today in front of the Art institute of Chicago were donated by Mrs. Henry (Annie) Field. Sculptor Edward Kemeys (1843-1907) designed and cast them.

Q: Where was the lions' first home?
A: Behind the Palace of Fine Arts at the Columbian Exposition.

1897

The cast bronze clock on the State and Washington corner of Marshall Field & Company was put into place. It was hung more than 17 feet above the ground and weighed nearly eight tons.

1898

The Chicago Public Library opened its new building at Randolph and Michigan in January.

Q: Who designed the new library?
A: The Boston firm of Shepley, Rutan and Coolidge, the same firm that had designed the Art Institute of Chicago.

1904

Alta Vista Terrace opened just east of Graceland Cemetery. In 1971 it was designated as Chicago's first historic district.

Q: Inspired by row houses developer Samuel Gross had seen in London, the homes on Alta Vista have one particularly startling characteristic. What is it?
A: The series of buildings on one side of the street exactly match that on the other. One series begins on the north end and the other on the south so that only in the middle of the block do matching houses face each other.

Q: Before building Alta Vista, Gross was spectacularly successful developing middle-class housing. He did all but which of the following?

1. Built 21 suburbs.
2. Constructed over 10,000 houses.
3. Sold more than 40,000 lots.
4. Billed himself as "The World's Greatest Real Estate Promoter."
5. Wrote a play called *The Merchant of Cornville,* which he claimed Edmund Rostand had plagiarized in writing Cyrano de Bergerac.

A: All of the above. Though Gross won a 1902 plagiarism suit against the French playwright, Rostand dismissed his claim as absurd.

1904

The Chicago Building went up on the southwest corner of what would become Chicago's main axis—State and Madison. Designed by the firm of

Holabird and Roche, it included two lessons for Chicago architecture buffs—Sullivan's basic concepts for skyscraper design and the famed Chicago window.

Q: How does the Chicago Building illustrate Sullivan's concepts?
A: Sullivan said tall buildings needed three elements: a base, a shaft, and a top. The decorative base—best illustrated by Sullivan's Carson Pirie Scott doorway across the street—anchors the building. Each floor of the shaft repeats itself to give the building vertical grace, and the top, usually a protruding cornice of some type, says stop, and this is where the building ends.

Q: What is a Chicago window?
A: The Chicago window, illustrated on the Chicago Building in both its flat and bay versions, had three elements: a large center stationary pane and two side windows that opened. The large window let in light, and the small ones let in air.

1908

The Hirsch, Stein & Company fertilizer warehouse was the world's first flat-slab concrete building.

1909

Daniel Burnham was commissioned to create the *Plan of Chicago,* the first comprehensive plan done for any major American city. Two of its significant aspects were keeping the Lake Michigan shoreline open for future generations and building a downtown that would rival London or Paris. Though they had competed with each other in establishing the military bases at Fort Sheridan and Great Lakes, the Merchant and Commercial Clubs got together to sponsor this plan.

Q: As the extant Commercial Club gets more credit for the plan than does the Merchants Club, which later merged into it, other major contributors didn't get the credit Daniel Burnham does for it. An architect and an artist both deserve note. Who are they?
A: Edward Bennett, Burnham's assistant, was coauthor of the plan; in the 1930s, he would be responsible for the elegant plans for Grant Park. Artist Jules Guerin prepared the lush illustrations, one of the plan's most remarkable aspects.

Q: Another remarkable Chicagoan who contributed to the plan's success was brewer Charles Wacker. What was his contribution?
A: As the first chair of the Chicago Plan Commission, Wacker worked ceaselessly to sell the plan to business and civic leaders, as well as to the

city at large. In addition to promotional movies about it shown in nick-elodeons, a textbook called *Wacker's Manual of the Plan of Chicago* was published in 1912. City schoolchildren were required to pass an exam based on it.

Q: Part of the *Plan of Chicago* appears as a trompe l'oeil on the side of a building along a major expressway near the Loop. Where is it and who painted it?

A: It is on the north side of the Eisenhower Expressway just west of Halsted. The artist's name is Richard Haas, and he is responsibile for sev-eral other trompe l'oeil murals in the city.

1911

Villa Turicum, with 44 rooms on 269 acres in Lake Forest, was built. It was torn down in 1956 without ever having been occupied.

Q: Villa Turicum was built to revive a failing marriage linking two of America's greatest commercial dynasties. Name the husband and wife and the dynasties.

A: Edith Rockefeller McCormick was the daughter of Standard Oil mag-nate John D. Rockefeller. Harold McCormick was the son of reaper king Cyrus McCormick.

1911

A. Montgomery Ward won the fourth and final lawsuit in his 20-year cam-paign to keep the Chicago lakefront "free and clear" of any buildings whatso-ever.

Q: What monument to Ward and his effort was recently erected, and where is it?

A: In 1994 the park fronting Michigan Avenue between Randolph and Madison Streets was named the A. Montgomery Ward Garden. A bust of Ward was placed in the park right across from the old Montgomery Ward headquarters building.

1915

Mayor William Hale Thompson, most often remembered as a buffoon, was also a builder. His election in 1915 saw the city embark on a building cam-paign that implemented many *Plan of Chicago* recommendations.

Q: All but which of the following projects opened during his administration?

1. The Michigan Avenue Bridge.
2. Soldier Field.
3. The elevation of 12th Street (now Roosevelt Road).
4. Wacker Drive.

A: Number 2. Soldier Field was opened in 1924 during the administration of William Dever, who was mayor between Thompson's first and second administrations. The colonnaded stadium was named in honor of America's WWI soldiers. At the same time, the Municipal Pier was renamed to honor sailors, becoming Navy Pier.

1916

Envisioned as one of five piers that would extend out into the lake, the Municipal Pier opened at the foot of Illinois Street. Combining both recreational and docking needs, it became obsolete when trucking replaced shipping as the primary means of delivering goods.

Q: What other purposes has the pier served?
A: During WWII it was used as a naval training facility, and for two decades it served as the Chicago Branch of the University of Illinois. In 1976 after modest renovation, it hosted Taste of Chicago. The pier reopened to new uses after a major renovation completed in 1995.

Q: How far out into the lake does the pier extend?
A: From the entrance building on the shore to the ballroom at its eastern end is a full half mile.

1916

Patrician Howard Van Doren Shaw was in his day the residential architect of choice for Chicago's elite. Among other clients, the village of Lake Forest hired him to design Market Square, its tony downtown shopping center.

Q: Shaw designed many classy buildings. What are some of the others.
A: The Lakeside Press Building at 731 South Plymouth Court (1897), Fourth Presbyterian Church at 125 East Chestnut Street (1912), the Quadrangle Club at the University of Chicago (1921), and the Goodman Memorial Theater (1925).

1921

On May 23 the Field Museum of Natural History opened its new building by the lake, five years, nine months, and seven days after construction had begun.

Q: Where did the two elephants in Stanley Field Hall of the Field Museum come from, who acquired them, and when?

A: They were collected in 1905 in British East Africa by the museum's chief taxidermist, Carl Akeley, and his wife, Delia. She, incidentally, shot the larger elephant herself.

Q: Why is the deer diorama "The Four Seasons" at the Field Museum world famous?

A: It was made by Akeley, considered the father of modern taxidermy, and is generally regarded as the first full-habitat diorama ever created.

1920

The socially prominent architect Benjamin Marshall built himself a playboy-like castle on Lake Michigan in Wilmette that featured tropical birds, an indoor swimming pool, and a permanent crew of young ladies.

Q: What buildings did Marshall make his money on?

A: The Drake Hotel, 999 North Lake Shore Drive, and 1515 North State Parkway among others.

Q: The playful Marshall was fond of driving home along Sheridan Road and devised a vehicle to make the experience even more fun. What was it?

A: He made Chicago's first convertible by removing the roof of his roadster.

1922

The *Chicago Tribune* announced a contest to design its new headquarters, attracting 189 designs from around the world. The panel unanimously agreed on the winner—the New York firm of Howells & Hood.

Q: Who came in second?

A: Eliel Saarinen. Walter Gropius also lost. The Finnish Saarinen would later have an impact on the city: 333 North Michigan Avenue was inspired by his tower entry.

1922

Lorado Taft's stupendous sculpture, *The Fountain of Time,* was dedicated at the western end of the Midway Plaisance. It was the most monumental piece he created in a long and distinguished career. Other Taft pieces include two of Graceland Cemetery's most striking grave markers: *The Crusader* (a memorial for *Daily News* publisher Victor Lawson) and *Eternal Silence* (a memorial for hotelier Dexter Graves), as well as *The Fountain of the Great Lakes* in the Art Institute's South Court.

Q: What piece of poetry inspired *The Fountain of Time?*
A: A line that read "Time goes, you say? Ah, no / Alas, time stays; we go," in "The Paradox of Time" by Austin Dobson.

Q: In 1911 another Taft piece was unveiled along the Illinois River. What was it and where is it located?
A: A tribute to the Native Americans who once inhabited the area, the statue called *Black Hawk* stands high above the river near Oregon, Illinois. The site a century ago of an artist's colony called Eagle's Nest, the surrounding area is now owned by the University of Illinois.

1923

Chicago enacted its first comprehensive zoning law, which was designed to discourage canyons downtown and encourage residential developments centered at major intersections in outlying areas.

Q: What distinctly Chicagoan residential areas developed partially as a result of this law?
A: When major intersections were designated for commercial use, areas of sturdy one-story brick homes grew up around them. These compact and easily expandable bungalows became Chicago's most representative style of residential building. They also used up the bricks manufactured here in great quantities.

1924

In this one year 16,253 buildings were erected in Chicago, taking up enough frontage to stretch from Chicago to Milwaukee (90.4 miles).

1924

Soldier Field opened on October 9.

1924

Edward Bennett, the same man who had helped Burnham write *The Plan of Chicago,* completed the layout for Grant Park.

Q: Grant Park, in common with much of Chicago's lakefront, is principally landfill. Where did the dirt for the fill come from?

A: Initially debris from the Chicago fire and numerous building projects was used. Later, dirt excavated during the digging of the Loop's extensive system—the same tunnels that flooded so disastrously in the spring of 1992—was dumped in Grant Park.

1927

Buckingham Fountain, donated by Kate Buckingham in memory of her brother, was dedicated on August 26. To this day it pushes 14,000 gallons of water a minute through 133 jets.

1929

The statue of Ceres atop the Board of Trade Building was put in place. It stood 31.5 feet high and weighed six tons.

Q: Who was its sculptor, and who is Ceres anyway?
A: He was John Storrs, a prominent sculptor who was very active in Chicago during the 1920s and 1930s. A model of it is on display at the Art Institute. Ceres, not coincidentally, was the Roman goddess of grain.

I want less of steers and less of pork, and more of culture.
EMERY STORRS, A PROMINENT ATTORNEY,
DURING AN ADDRESS IN 1881

1929

The Merchandise Mart, with 97 acres of floor space, more than twice that of its nearest competitor, became the world's largest commercial building when it opened just before the October stock market crash.

Q: Statues of eight famous merchants line the driveway of the Merchandise Mart. Name them.
A: Marshall Field, George Huntington Hartford, John R. Wanamaker, Frank Woolworth, Edward A. Filene, Julius Rosenwald, General Robert E. Wood, and A. Montgomery Ward.

Q: What famous American businessman bought the Merchandise Mart for a song just after World War II?
A: Joseph P. Kennedy. The Kennedy family still owns it today.

1933

The Museum of Science and Industry opened in the old Palace of Fine Arts in Jackson Park with a gift of $3 million from Sears, Roebuck Chairman Julium Rosenwald.

Charity is the one pleasure that never wears out.
JULIUS ROSENWALD, PHILANTHROPIST

Q: Two other museums had been in that space. What were they?
A: Originally it was built for the Columbian Exposition. Then for nearly 25 years it was home to the Field Museum of Natural History.

Q: One of the museum's most affectionately regarded exhibits is the neither scientific nor industrial Fairy Castle, which was built by Colleen Moore. Who was she, and how did the house come to be at the museum?
A: Moore grew up in the south and became a major silent screen star in Hollywood with the help of *Front Page* editor Walter Howey—her uncle. She married a Chicago stockbroker and used her free time to complete her elaborate dollhouse, which she'd begun as a child. She gave it to the museum in 1949.

1933

During the height of the depression, homeless people across the country built shantytowns known as "Hoovervilles." Chicago's biggest one was below Michigan Avenue and Wacker Drive, which was still under construction at that time. Some 2,000 homeless people lived there.

1935

Katherine Kuh opened her gallery in Diana Court on Michigan Avenue. The only Chicago gallery specializing in Modernist works of art, it rapidly became nationally known and helped launch Kuh's career as art critic for the *Saturday Review of Books*.

1937

Josephine Hancock Logan, patroness of the arts and a major donor to the Art Institute, founded the Sanity in Art Movement to "rid museums of moronic grotesqueries that masquerade as art."

Q: Logan and her husband endowed the Logan Medal to promote excellence in art. What famous painting in the Art Institute was awarded the Logan Medal and aroused Logan's never ending ire?
A: *American Gothic* by Grant Wood.

Many of the finest artists in Chicago had had their works rejected ... while immature and meaningless works of their pupils were accepted.... There [is]

no valid reason for abstract or picture puzzles in art, nor any disturbed figures or unnatural landscapes.
JOSEPHINE HANCOCK LOGAN, 1937

Sanity in art—sanity in everything—is indeed a fine goal at which to aim; but the question immediately arises: whose sanity?
CHAUNCEY MCCORMICK, A MEMBER OF THE ART
INSTITUTE'S BOARD OF TRUSTEES AT THE TIME

1937

Ludwig Mies van der Rohe and Laszlo Moholy-Nagy, former faculty members of the original Bauhaus in Germany, arrived in Chicago as refugees from Hitler's Europe. Despite the fact that they mightily disliked each other, they headed schools that a decade later were both part of the new Illinois Institute of Technology.

Q: Moholy-Nagy's new Bauhaus in Chicago lasted only one year, in part because of opposition from Mies. What name did the school Moholy established eventually become known as?

A: With substantial support from Walter and Elizabeth Paepcke—founders of the trend-setting Container Corporation of America and of Aspen, Colorado—it became the Institute of Design, which merged into IIT in 1947.

Let this building be the home of ideas and adventure [that would be] in the end a real contribution to our civilization.
LUDWIG MIES VAN DER ROHE AT THE DEDICATION
OF IIT'S CROWN HALL IN 1956

Q: Mies van der Rohe's work reflected the 20-century's obsession with technology and industry. Name three of his buildings in Chicago.

A: Among them are the Promontory Apartments at 5530 South Shore Drive, twin apartment buildings at 860-880 North Lake Shore Drive, Crown Hall on the IIT campus, the Federal Center at Jackson and Dearborn, and the IBM Building on North Wabash.

1955

After a 20-year lull, office building construction got going again in downtown Chicago. The 40-story Prudential Building, completed that year, became the city's tallest.

Q: A restaurant at its summit was once a classy place to have dinner. Why was it called the Top of the Rock?

A: The Prudential Insurance Company used the Rock of Gibraltar in its advertising campaigns. Created by famed sculptor Alfonso Ianelli with Frank Lloyd Wright as collaborator, a sculptured relief on the building's western facade celebrates that rock.

1965

Marina City opened, quickly becoming the most photographed building in the city, if not the country. The design was revolutionary in several ways. The two corncob-shaped towers included both parking and living spaces. The circular access to the former was unique, and the pie shape of the latter made the apartments feel larger than they were.

Q: The idea behind the building was "a city within a city," offering a stark contrast to the suburbs to which many city residents were escaping. What else did the complex consist of when built?
A: There was not only a grocery store and dry cleaners, but a restaurant, health club, swimming pool, skating rink, theater, marina, bowling alley, and office building.

Architects were the only creative professionals who didn't have to apologize for staying in Chicago.
BERTRAND GOLDBERG, MARINA CITY ARCHITECT

1968

Lake Point Tower, still the world's tallest purely residential building, opened on Lake Shore Drive near Navy Pier.

Q: What was the building's design inspiration?
A: In 1921 Mies van der Rohe envisioned an asymmetrical glass-walled building. Two of his former students at IIT designed it shortly after Mies's death in 1967.

Q: What Chicago-based architectural innovation is amply demonstrated at Lake Point Tower?
A: The curtain wall. Until Chicago architects invented steel-frame construction in the 1880s, a building's exterior walls held up the weight of its interior spaces. When steel-framing was introduced, this interior structure carried the building's weight and left the external wall to be nothing more than a "curtain." The undulating glass exterior of Lake Point Tower is such a wall.

1969

The First National Bank of Chicago Building opened. It was another tapering structure like the Hancock Building.

Q: Aesthetics weren't the sole reason for its shape, either. What was the other?

A: Illinois banking laws decreed that all of a bank's offices and services had to be under one roof. As a result, the public spaces for the building took up nearly a square block while the offices for the bank and tenants required less space as the building rose.

1971

Woodfield Mall, the world's largest shopping mall, was opened in Schaumburg.

Q: How was the name Woodfield derived?

A: From Robert E. *Wood*, of Sears, Roebuck and Marshall *Field*.

1973

The Sears Tower was topped out on May 3. At 1,468 feet and 110 stories, it remained the tallest building in the world until 1996, when a building in Kuala Lompour eclipsed it by a few feet.

Q: Three Chicago buildings are still among the world's tallest. Besides the Sears Tower, which are they?

A: The Amoco Building (1973) is Chicago's second tallest and the John Hancock Center (1969) is the city's third tallest.

Q: What is the purpose of the Hancock's tapering form?

A: It's not just to remind folks of obelisks or the Washington Monument. It has a very commercial justification. It provides large floor areas for retail spaces and offices on the lower floors and smaller areas above for condominiums.

Q: An architect and an engineer at the firm of Skidmore, Owings, and Merrill were responsible for the Sears Tower and the John Hancock Center. Who were they?

A: Bruce Graham was chief architect, and structural engineer Fazlur Khan is credited with devising the design that enables the buildings to stand so tall.

1976

Led by fanciful architect Stanley Tigerman, the Chicago chapter of the American Institute of Architects sponsored a show called "Late Entries in the Tribune Tower Competition." The liveliness of the resulting entries—Tigerman's was a Miesian skyscraper sinking into the lake—drew new attention to Chicago's architectural heritage, both in the city and around the country.

1976

Led by art dealer Roberta Lieberman, many Michigan Avenue galleries began moving into a dying warehouse district along Franklin and Orleans Streets south of Chicago Avenue. It signaled the start of a burgeoning new art district and a rehabilitation of an aging neighborhood now known as River North.

Q: In 1989 a disaster hit Lieberman's gallery and several others. What was it?
A: The block-square loft building that housed eight galleries, undergoing substantial renovation at the time, burned to the ground, creating a temporary setback in the area's growth.

1981

On May 25, wearing a skintight Spiderman costume, Daniel Goodwin, a mountain climber and actor, was the first person to scale the outside of the 110-story Sears Tower. He made his ascent on May 25, 1981, with a ladder to the first floor. He used suction cups and straps to travel the 1,454 feet in just under seven and a half hours. In preparation for the climb he ran, lifted weights, and ate little or no meat. His diet included grain and lots of sea algae. The costume cost him $450.

Q: What other Chicago building did Goodwin climb?
A: In November 1981 Spiderman Goodwin tried to climb the John Hancock Center, only to have city fireman pour water on him in an attempt to stop him, which prompted one onlooker to remark, "That was the most stupid thing I ever saw."

1992

The collection in the Field Museum's storage vaults had grown to 19,430,005 biological specimens, 9,886,646 of which were insects.

1992

The Harold Washington Library Center opened at State and Congress and became the world's largest municipal building.

1995

The Prairie Avenue Bookshop, founded in 1975 on South Dearborn Street, moved to a new location on South Wabash and won acclaim from London as "the best architectural bookshop in the world."

1996

The world's largest waste water treatment plant remains the West-Southwest plant in Stickney, which treats 800 million gallons a day, according to the Metropolitan Water Reclamation District of Greater Chicago. It was designed to treat up to 1.2 billion gallons a day.

CHAPTER 8

Dancing on the Volcano

I adore Chicago. It is the pulse of America.

ACTRESS SARAH BERNHARDT, 1881

Chicago is an ideal location for dancing on top of a volcano. Eruptive and exciting, a city of superlatives. It exaggerates all the splendor and squalor in America.

ANNE O'HARE MCCORMICK, A JOURNALIST
IN NEW YORK, 1932

Why in the world does the city not cut its New York apron strings and itself produce plays for Chicago and the Middle West?

CRITIC EDWARD WAGENKNECHT, COMMENTING
ON HIS HOMETOWN IN 1964

Leader that it has been in other fields of endeavor, Chicago has often been indifferent—and at times overtly hostile—to the performing arts. Indeed, it has only been in the past 20 years that Chicago has become known as a center for performers of all stripes.

The cause of this indifference was the same boisterousness that gave Chicago so much character in the late 19th century. People scrambling to get rich either don't have time to go to public entertainments, or if they do, they often prefer performances a little—shall we say—livelier than the traditional highbrow variety. So it was in Chicago, which early on became a center for dance music, jazz, blues, nightclubs, spectacles, and scantily clad women. Classical music and legitimate theater were present, but not central to the Chicago experience.

Ironically, it was only after Chicago stopped booming that the performing arts had time to catch up. The true flowering of Chicago's performing arts began slowly after World War II and accelerated in the 1970s, when Chicagoans suddenly awoke to find themselves with a world-renowned symphony orchestra and opera company, as well as a theater community that was making headlines across the country.

The opposition went away as well. Chicago's mayors have seldom been known for their cultural aspirations, and Richard J. Daley was no exception. Daley failed to see the arts as crucial to the city's future. When he died in 1976, his successor, Michael Bilandic, soon married the socialite he'd appointed to be the city's first fine arts commissioner.

No history of arts in Chicago would be complete without mention of Claudia Cassidy, the acerbic music and theater critic of the *Chicago Tribune*. For over two decades, from the 1940s to 1965, her high standards caused her to so routinely lambast performers that many just stopped coming to town.

Today, however, Chicago finds itself second only to New York as the nation's center for the performing arts. And Chicago is second to no city in the world for its supply of those two quintessentially American music forms, blues and jazz.

1818

Fiddle-playing free spirit Mark Beaubien joined his fur-trading brother Jean-Baptiste in Chicago and the two opened the Sauganash Hotel at the point where the Chicago River branches south. Led by these Creole Beaubien brothers, dance and drink democratized the wild settlement growing up around Wolf Point. The father of 23 children, brother Mark was to say of those early days, "Oh, them was fine times...never come anymore."

I plays de fiddle like de debble, an I keeps hotel like hell.
        MARK BEAUBIEN, CHICAGO'S FIRST INNKEEPER IN 1830

1834

The village of Chicago hosted its first magic show on February 24. It was described as an "entertainment of legerdemain and ventriloquism" by a Mr. Bowers, who performed it. The performance was held at a mansion on Lake Street. Admission was 50 cents for adults and 25 cents for children.

1834

The first piano was brought to Chicago by John-Baptiste Beaubien. Business had apparently outgrown his brother's single fiddle.

1837

Joseph Jefferson, the noted American actor and playwright, appeared for the first time in Chicago with his parents.

Q: Why is Joseph Jefferson's name familiar in Chicago today?
A: The annual excellence awards for Chicago theater are named after him and his father, also a noted actor. Jefferson's signature play, which he wrote and starred in, was *Rip Van Winkle*.

1838

The first regular theater in Chicago history, the Rialto, opened on Dearborn Street between Lake and South Water (now Wacker Drive).

1850

On July 30 *La Sonnambula* was the first opera performed in Chicago—after a fashion. As Act Two began the theater caught on fire and burned to the ground.

1857

James H. McVicker spent $85,000 to build a theater on Madison Street. Three more theaters offering live entertainment would be built on that site. In 1922 the last was pulled down to be replaced by a movie palace.

Chicago's contributions to the Union's victory in the Civil War included those of the composer and publisher of its most popular songs, George F. Root. His "The Battle Cry of Freedom" became the unofficial marching song of the Union army.

> *Yes, we'll rally round the flag boys, We'll rally once again. Shouting the Battle Cry of Freedom.*
>
> George F. Root

Q: What were some of Root's other popular war songs?
A: There were several. The most well known are "Just Before the Battle Mother" and "Tramp, Tramp, Tramp." A popular writer of gospel hymns, Root, his brother, and a friend started Root and Cady, a leading publisher of sheet music.

1862

A noted actor from a famous thespian family made his first Chicago appearances in January playing in *Richard III* and *The Merchant of Venice* at the McVickers. John Wilkes Booth then became famous for a less-admirable endeavor.

1865

On April 15 the opening of Crosby's Opera House was canceled out of respect for President Lincoln, whom Booth had assassinated the day before.

1867

A musician named Florenz Ziegfield established the Chicago Academy of Music four years after arriving from Germany.

Q: Ziegfield's son—also named Florenz—went on to establish the Ziegfield Follies and become an American institution. Where did he get his start as a producer?

A: He, too, worked at the Columbian Exposition, showcasing a band from Germany, singers from Russia, an orchestra from Hungary, and a well-endowed young athlete named Eugene Sandow, whom he billed as "the Perfect Man."

1872

Impresario Richard Healey opened Powers Theater on Randolph. It would be regarded as Chicago's classiest theater until the Blackstone opened in 1910

> *Oh, Sodom was some and Gomorrah was great,*
> *And in Venice each man's an Iago.*
> *But nothing out there can ever compare*
> *With the sweet state of things in Chicago.*
>> A SONG LYRIC POPULAR AFTER THE CIVIL WAR

1881

Sarah Bernhardt arrived in Chicago to play Phedre and Camille. Some members of the city's Protestant aristocracy decreed that her shows were too provocative for proper people to attend. She apparently was not offended.

1882

Henrik Ibsen's *Ghosts,* banned throughout Europe for its treatment of venereal disease, received its world premiere in Chicago—in Norwegian—with Helga von Bluhme as Mrs. Alving.

1891

Theodore Thomas, past director of the New York Philharmonic, accepted an invitation to head Chicago's fledgling Orchestral Association. Among his innovations were popular workingmen's concerts, which he started in 1893.

I would go to Hell if they would give me a permanent orchestra.
THEODORE THOMAS, WHO HADN'T HAD ONE WHILE IN NEW YORK

Q: What was the orchestra's first home?
A: The Auditorium Theater, where it played until Orchestra Hall was built in 1905.

Q: The Chicago Symphony has had just nine musical directors. Name them.
A: Theodore Thomas, Frederick Stock, Desire Defauw, Rafael Kubelik, Artur Rodzinski, Fritz Reiner, Jean Martinon, Sir Georg Solti, and Daniel Barenboim.

1900

Famed English actress Ellen Terry stopped in Chicago on an American tour. Her friend, the playwright George Bernard Shaw, offered a comment on the city before her arrival.

Chicago is a comparatively enlightened town; my plays get good houses there.
GEORGE BERNARD SHAW

1902

Chicago developer Samuel Eberly Gross won a plagiarism suit against Edmond Rostand, claiming the latter stole the play *Cyrano de Bergerac* from Gross's own work, *The Merchant Prince of Cornville*.

1903

Chicago police chief Francis O'Neil published the seminal *O'Neil's Music of Ireland*. The Irish-born flute player had settled in Chicago in 1873, joined the police force and, upon retirement in 1905, devoted nearly 30 more years to studying Irish music.

1904

The worst theater fire in the nation's history happened when 603 people, including 212 children, were trapped in the burning Iroquois Theater during a holiday matinee. The red "Exit" lights in all public places—and doors that open out—are a result of that disaster.

1904

Ravinia Park opened on August 15. Originally established as a means of encouraging area residents to ride electric trains serving the park, it quickly became an institution and the Chicago Symphony Orchestra's summer home.

1910

The Chicago Grand Opera Company was established. Its dynamic and entertaining diva, Mary Garden, originated some of her most popular and controversial roles there. Among them was Salome, which she performed in a sensual fashion that appalled some conservative opera patrons.

> *I am a normal man, but I would not trust myself to see* Salome.
> ARTHUR FARWELL, A PRESIDENT OF THE LAW AND ORDER LEAGUE,
> AND A MEMBER OF LAKE FOREST'S FOUNDING FAMILY

Q: Garden pioneered in another role that Carol Fox and Ardis Krainik later played as well. What was it?

A: In 1921 Garden became the first woman to run an opera company, a role both Fox and Krainik assumed later.

> *I began at the top, I stayed at the top, and I quit at the top.*
> MARY GARDEN, UPON HER RETIREMENT

1912

A city ordinance declared Maxwell Street, which had attracted Jewish immigrants for decades, an open-air market, and it quickly became a magnet for blues musicians.

> *There'd be musicians lined all up and down the street. So this was where the music world began, right there on Maxwell Street, among us. Which was mostly where they turned pro, right there on Maxwell Street every Sunday.*
> MUSICIAN JOHNNY WILLIAMS

1912

The Little Theater was established in a small auditorium of the Fine Arts Building on South Mighigan Avenue to produce avant-garde works neglected by larger commercial theaters.

1915

A kid born on Maxwell Street named Barney Balaban joined up with Sam Katz to open a classy theater on Central Park Avenue. Its mix of stage shows and movies was a hit, and the pair soon opened several others, including the Riviera, the Granada, and in 1921 the Chicago Theatre.

Q: Twenty years later a talented vaudeville performer named Lester worked for the Balaban & Katz organization as a set and costume designer. He

would go on to direct dozens of significant films and marry Judy
Garland after she starred in Chicagoan L. Frank Baum's *Wizard of Oz*.
What was the stage name this man used?

A: Vincente Minnelli. When he was a kid, his impoverished family had an
act called the Minnelli Brothers Tent Theater.

1921

The Chicago Theater opened at State and Lake on October 26 with the film
The Sign in the Door.

1922

Louisiana trumpeter Louis Armstrong, among others, brought New Orleans-
style jazz to Chicago and made the city the jazz capital of the world.

Q: How did Armstrong happen to come to Chicago?

A: New Orleans jazz cornetist Joe "King" Oliver hired Armstrong to play
with his jazz band at the Lincoln Gardens Theater on East 31st Street.

*It was an accident that swing and I were born and brought up side by side
in New Orleans, traveled up the Mississippi together and, in 1922, were
there in Chicago, getting acquainted with the North, and the North getting
acquainted with us.*

LOUIS ARMSTRONG

Q: Armstrong is also credited with developing the school of jazz singing in
which sounds and phrases are used instead of words. What is it called?

A: Scat.

Q: What is Chicago jazz?

A: A style modeled after the great African-American jazz musicians but
marked by a fluent and strong rhythmic beat.

*If you want to play real jazz, go live close to the Negro, see through his eyes,
laugh and cry with him, soak up his spirit.*

MEZZ MEZZROW, CLARINETIST AND SAXMAN IN
HIS AUTOBIOGRAPHY, *REALLY THE BLUES*

1922

Lester Melrose, a white businessman, opened a music store on the South Side
and was the first to publish works by Jelly Roll Morton and Joe "King" Oliver.

1923

Earl "Fatha" Hines got his first gig in Chicago at the Elite Club at State and 30th Streets. Later, he moved to the famed Grand Terrace Ballroom at 39th Street and Grand Boulevard (now Martin Luther King Drive.)

Earl Hines … was a man whose music not only tested the rules but left us in doubt as to whether there were any rules, other than the ones his inspiration managed to create.
Jazz critic Larry Kart, upon Hines's death in 1983

Q: Hines was famous for helping launch other musicians' careers. Name some of them.
A: Dizzy Gillespie, Charlie Parker, Billy Eckstine, and Sarah Vaughan, among others.

1923

With firms like Kimball and Lyon & Healy, Chicago had become a leading center of piano manufacturing. In this one year, the industry used 800 tons of glue and 220,000 gallons of varnish, as well as countless trees to make these pianos.

1927

"Liza," "Nobody's Sweetheart," "China Boy," and "Sugar" were recorded by Gene Krupa, Frank Teschemacher, Jimmy McPartland, Bud Freeman, Joe Sullivan, Jim Lannigan, and Eddie Condon. The takes are today regarded as the epitome of Chicago-style jazz.

1931

The leaders of the Pilgrim Baptist Church on South Indiana Avenue gave their organist permission to begin using a new style of church music. His name was Thomas A. Dorsey, and the music he introduced became world famous as gospel music.

Q: What was Dorsey's greatest hit?
A: "Take My Hand, Precious Lord," which he wrote while recovering from the loss of his wife and baby daughter during childbirth.

Q: Gospel great Mahalia Jackson was known for all but which of the following?

1. She sang the National Anthem at JFK's funeral.
2. She began her career with Mahalia's beauty shop on South Indiana.

3. She made the first gospel record to sell a million copies.

4. She is buried in Oak Lawn cemetery.

A: All but number 4. Jackson is buried in New Orleans.

Q: Which record of Jackson's sold a million copies?

A: "Move On Up a Little Higher," which she recorded in 1947 on the Apollo label.

1933

Sally Rand danced behind just two ostrich feathers to pack in male spectators at the Century of Progress Fair. Her act was broken up four times daily by the police, and she wound up earning $3,000 a week.

Q: What was Sally Rand's real name?

A: Born Helen Gould Beck, she changed her name while under contract to C. B. DeMille. She chose Rand because DeMille was reading a Rand McNally atlas at the time that he interviewed her.

If you ask me, they are just a lot of boobs come to see a woman wiggle with a fan or without fig leaves. But we have boobs and we have a right to cater to them.

JUDGE JOSEPH B. DAVID, WHO TRIED SALLY RAND

I haven't been without work a day since I took off my pants.

SALLY RAND

1933

A young man from Wicker Park introduced flame dancers at the Century of Progress exposition. Twenty-five years later, after producing *Around the World in Eighty Days* and marrying Elizabeth Taylor, he returned to Chicago to be buried in Waldheim Cemetery.

Q: Avrom Hirsch Goldbogen was his name at birth. What name do we know this famous producer by?

A: Michael Todd. He died at age 51 in a New Mexico plane crash.

1934

John Lee "Jonny boy" Williamson arrived in Chicago with his blues harmonica. His playing helped shape Chicago blues until his early death in 1948.

1935

A thriving community eventually known as Bronzeville was established along 35th Street and shortly extended down State Street to 47th. The center of Chicago's rapidly expanding black community, it attracted writers and entertainers from around the country.

Q: What theater was central to this community and where is it now?

A: The Regal Theater on 47th Street attracted top black entertainers from the 1930s through the 1950s, then fell on hard times as the surrounding neighborhood deteriorated. In the late 1980s the former Avalon Theater on 79th Street, an exuberant moorish fantasy, was redone to become the New Regal Theater.

1936

The first public performance by a radically integrated musical ensemble occurred in Chicago when Benny Goodman, Gene Krupa, Lionel Hampton, and Teddy Wilson played the Congress Hotel.

Q: Benny Goodman is known for all but which of the following?

1. He was a high school dropout from the Maxwell Street ghetto.
2. He changed the course of popular music, becoming known as the "King of Swing."
3. He was the first white musician to utilize black talent.
4. He was popular with and loyal to the musicians he played with.
5. He got his start playing in a Hull House street band.

A: All but number 4. He was notoriously difficult to get along with, but he did remain loyal and generous to Hull House.

Q: One of Chicago's most famous jazz group of the 1930s was the Austin High Gang. Who was in it?

A: Bud Freeman on saxophone, Jimmy McPartland on cornet, Dick McPartland on guitar, Jim Lannigan on bass, Frank Teschemacher on alto sax and clarinet, Dave North on piano, and Dave Tough on drums. Benny Goodman occasionally sat in.

Q: Where did the name of the group come from?

A: Most of its members had actually attended Austin High School on the West Side.

1939

The song "Chicago" was first sung in the movie *The Story of Vernon and Irene Castle.*

Q: In addition to Frank Sinatra, how many performers have recorded "Chicago"?
A: At least 18, including Count Basie, Tony Bennett, Eddie Condon, Jimmy Dorsey, Tommy Dorsey, Judy Garland, Benny Goodman, Stephane Grappelli, Jimmie Grier, Coleman Hawkins, Earl Hines, Al Hirt, Stan Mark, Billy May and the Orchestra, Memphis Slim, the Original Piano trio, Django Reinhardt, and Mugsy Spanier.

1940

A one-way ticket from New Orleans to Chicago on the Illinois Central Railroad—the most common route for Negro musicians heading north— cost $16.95.

1942

James C. Petrillo, the Chicago-bred-and-based president of the American Federation of Musicians, forced a two-year shutdown of the recording industry until musicians began receiving jukebox and broadcast royalties.

Q: A decade earlier, the combative Petrillo had initiated another means of making sure musicians got paid. What was it?
A: The introduction of talking films had put nearly 2,000 musicians out of work just as the depression hit, so the Chicago Park District and Petrillo's union local joined together to start the Grant Park Concerts.

Q: How is Petrillo remembered today?
A: The Grant Park band shell is named after him.

1943

In May McKinley Morganfield arrived in Chicago from Clarksdale, Mississippi, on the Illinois Central Railroad. He changed his name to Muddy Waters and became the most famous blues musician in Chicago's history.

Q: Muddy Waters did which of the following?

1. Didn't take up guitar until he was 17, a very late age for a blues singer.
2. Took his name from his habit of playing in a muddy creek near his home.

3. Recorded "I Can't Be Satisfied" (later made world famous in another version by the Rolling Stones) and "I Feel Like Going Home" in 1948 on the Chess Aristocrat label.

A: All of the above.

I always wanted to be great. I always wanted to be known cross-country, not like an ordinary person who just lives and dies.

MUDDY WATERS

Blues ain't nothin' but a good woman cryin' for her man.

OLD SAYING

1946

Two Polish-born brothers, Len and Phil Chess, started Aristocrat Records. The name was later changed to Chess Records and it became the most important label for blues music in the world.

Blues is nothing but the truth.

LEONARD AND PHIL CHESS

Q: Name some of the artists who recorded on the Chess label.
A: Muddy Waters, Howlin' Wolf, Robert Nighthawk, Jimmy Rogers, Little Walter, Sonny Boy Williamson, Johnny Shines, J. B. Lenoir, Willie Dixon, and the Rolling Stones.

Q: What white Chicago native played with the great black blues artists when he was still underage and went on to popularize blues for a rock audience before dying of a drug overdose at the age of 45?
A: Paul Butterfield.

1947

Studs Terkel began his "I Come for to Sing" folk music series at the Blue Note, a landmark Loop nightclub until it closed in the 1960s.

1949

Irna Phillips, the queen of radio soap-opera writers, saw her *Guiding Light* become the first serial adapted to television.

Q: Responsible for dozens of hit shows, Phillips did all her writing from what part of town?
A: Her apartment on Astor Street. None of her shows had settings remotely like that posh part of town.

1950

When Chicago-born Frankie LoVecchio started his climb to fame as a singer, he took the name of his high school, Lane Tech, and became Frankie Lane.

Q: For which television series did Frankie Lane sing the theme song?
A: *Rawhide.*

1954

The Lyric Opera of Chicago debuted with two performances of *Don Giovanni*.

Q: Maria Callas made her American debut in 1954 in a production that cemented the success of the newly formed Lyric Opera. What was the opera?
A: Bellini's *Norma*.

Q: What baritone who grew up in Downers Grove sang the Schlitz Beer tag before he became world famous?
A: Sherrill Milnes, who also taught at Northwestern University's music school.

1955

Charles Edward Berry, a.k.a. Chuck Berry, recorded "Maybelline" for the Chess label, and it quickly reached number one on the *Billboard* charts.

1956

Sidney Poitier, Ruby Dee, Diana Sands, Glynn Turner, Ivan Dixon, and Louis Gossett opened at the Blackstone Theater in *A Raisin in the Sun* by black Chicago writer Lorraine Hansberry.

1957

The Old Town School of Folk Music was founded by, among others, veteran Chicago singer and songwriter Win Stracke. It rapidly became the national center for the folk revival, and virtually every major folk artist has appeared there since.

Q: What seminal figure in the development of the Chicago Blues worked as a Pullman porter to support his music and left his guitar to the Old Town School when he died?
A: "Big" Bill Broonzy

Nobody gave us lessons. It was just born in us to sing and play the blues.
"Big" Bill Broonzy

1957

Sam Cooke became the first major gospel star to cross over to pop music. Until his tragic death at age 30 Cooke was one of the first black artists to enjoy widespread popularity among whites.

Q: Cooke had many hits, including "Everybody Loves to Cha-Cha," "Twistin' the Night Away," and "Another Saturday Night," but what was his first million-single seller?
A: "You Send Me."

1959

The Second City opened on December 16. It was—and remains—the country's premier improvisational comedy troupe.

Q: Who were the first producers of Second City?
A: Paul Sills, Bernie Sahlins, and Howard Alk.

Q: What was the name of the forerunner group of Second City, where was it located, and who was in it?
A: The Compass Players, founded in 1955 in Hyde Park. Among its members were Mike Nichols, Elaine May, Shelley Berman, Alan Arkin, Anne Meara, Ed Asner, Barbara Harris, Bernie Sahlins, Paul Sills, Jerry Stiller, and Viola Spolin.

1960

Famed Yiddish-theater star Dina Halpern, a Chicago resident since 1948, founded the Chicago Yiddish Theater Association, which lasted for ten years.

Q: Along with her husband, the ageless Lyric Opera publicist Danny Newman, Halpern contributed to what other Chicago resource?
A: Their extensive collection of materials on Judaica and Yiddish theater became the basis of a significant special collection in the Chicago Public Library.

1960

When asked to review the recent Chicago theater season, caustic *Chicago Tribune* critic Claudia Cassidy replied, "What season?" When her reign of terror finally ended in 1965, no one mourned.

1964

The Beatles made their Chicago debut at the International Amphitheater on September 5. They made $1,000 a minute for their show.

Q: While in town, the Beatles stayed in the Astor House, a novel Bertrand Goldberg building designed as a hotel. What similarly distinctive institution was housed in its basement?

A: Before there was an Elaine's, Chicago had Maxim's, an exact replica of the Paris original. Hostess Nancy Florsheim Goldberg acquainted tout le Chicago with classic French cuisine there.

1970

The Ruth Page Foundation School, one of the premier ballet training schools in the country, was opened by Ruth Page when she was 71 years old.

Q: The school is still operating. Where is it located?

A: It offers classes for both adults and children on Dearborn Street near Maple. Its theater is also home to the Shakespeare Repertory Company.

Q: Ruth Page did all but which of the following?

1. She was the first American to dance with the Ballet Russe.
2. She was a soloist at the Metropolitan Opera while still a teenager.
3. She started Chicago's first ballet company.
4. She choreographed a Chicago-inspired ballet called *Oak Street Beach*.

A: All but number 3. Page worked for years to get a ballet company started, to no avail.

I have learned from long experience that Chicago is the most difficult city to get things going in. Chicagoans are timid and don't trust their own taste, and they must be sure that they are approved every place else before they can accept it.
                                                                            RUTH PAGE

1979

Some historians date the beginning of the Chicago theater boom from this year, when the struggling Body Politic Theater agreed to share a theater space with the also-struggling Victory Gardens Theater.

Chicago is the mother lode for theater in this country.
                                                ACTRESS NAN MARTIN IN 1995

1984

Steve Goodman, Chicago's most endearing folk singer/writer, died of leukemia but not before having written dozens of songs about Chicago, including "Daley's Gone," "Go Cubs Go," "A Dying Cub Fan's Last Request," and "Lincoln Park Pirates."

Q: What was Steve Goodman's greatest hit and who recorded it?
A: "The City of New Orleans," which Arlo Guthrie made famous.

1990

The new Steppenwolf Theater opened on Halsted Street. While the *New York Times* carried a lengthy article on it, Chicago's two major newspapers gave more attention to the opening of *Ms. Saigon* on Broadway.

1993

Sir Georg Solti stepped down as musical director of the Chicago Symphony Orchestra. During his tenure, the CSO went from being merely a great orchestra to being one of the world's most acclaimed orchestras.

Q: Sir Georg Solti has won more Grammys with the Chicago Symphony than any other musician in history. How many?
A: Twenty-four.

Something extraordinary happened in Chicago. I made no changes, we didn't have to adjust to each other, our ways of making music were the same. Wine became champagne; we sparkled together. It's like Siegfried and Brunhilde. The girl was beautiful, and Siegfried turned out not to be impotent.
SIR GEORG SOLTI, ON THE SUCCESSES THE
CSO ENJOYED UNDER HIS BATON

1995

The Joffrey Ballet moved to Chicago.

Chicago hasn't been corroded with ultrasophistication and with its citizens esteeming of their own quality.
GERALD ARPINO, COFOUNDER OF THE
JOFFREY, ON ITS DECISION TO MOVE

CHAPTER 9

Lampposts in the Bleachers

I would rather be a lamp-post in Chicago than a million-aire in any other city.

WILLIAM HULBERT, FOUNDER OF THE
CHICAGO WHITE STOCKINGS

My friends are the fans, not the owners. Dignity isn't my suit of clothes.

BILL VEECK, TWO-TIME OWNER OF
THE CHICAGO WHITE SOX

Although Chicago has professional teams in every major sport, its championships have been few and far between. For example, the White Sox threw the 1919 World Series and then went 40 years before going back to a World Series, only to lose to the Los Angeles Dodgers. The Bears have won championships, as have the Black Hawks, but not very often, and as for the Cubs—well, the less said, the better. The Bulls, of course, are another story.

But Chicago is still a sporting town. Its fans are loyal, and on any given Sunday in the summer months, baseball diamonds and tennis courts across the city are filled with people doing sports their way. Add to these the amusement parks, bowling alleys, race tracks, and golf courses, and Chicago emerges as a place where people play, and play hard. The following makes that obvious.

As you read, keep in mind that no other field of human endeavor is so filled with trivia as the world of sports. To those die-hard sports fans who cannot live without knowing which National League left-handed pitcher holds the record for most odd-numbered innings pitched in away games during the month of July in even-numbered years, we refer you to the sports section of your local bookstore. What follows is, we freely confess, a mere sampling of Chicago's more interesting sports facts.

1839

The Chicago City Council prohibited billiard tables and nine-pin bowling alleys inside the city limits.

1870

In the nation's first intercity baseball game, the new Chicago White Stockings played a team from New Orleans. The record fails to show who won.

1875

Baseball mania struck Chicago with the velocity at which the city was growing, and Chicago's White Stockings signed up a young slugger from Iowa named Adrian Anson. Soon renamed "Cap" by his adoring fans, Anson led the team to win five National League pennants in seven years.

Q: Anson is also known for being all but which of the following?

1. The greatest 19th-century slugger.
2. The greatest 19th-century player/manager.
3. The first player to hit a home run in Comiskey Park.
4. The city clerk of Chicago from 1905 to 1907.
5. The coach who recruited runner, and later evangelist, Billy Sunday.

A: All but number 3. Comiskey Park wasn't built until after Anson had retired.

1876

The National League was formed with wealthy Chicago coal dealer William A. Hulbert, owner of the White Stockings team, serving as its first president.

1882

Hulbert died, leaving the White Stockings to cofounder and former player-manager, Albert G. (for Goodwill) Spalding. Staunch believers in the reserve clause, Hulbert and Spalding helped develop the notion that baseball players were the property of team owners.

In fighting the encroachments of drink upon the efficiency of individual players, we are simply striving to give our patrons the full measure of entertainment and satisfaction to which they are entitled.

ALBERT G. SPALDING, 1887

1884

The Washington Park Race Club opened, and it quickly drew Chicago's fashionable set. Founded under the leadership of Civil War general Philip Sheridan, the course was one of the country's finest thoroughbred racing tracks. It had a 10,000 seat grandstand and a clubhouse designed by Pullman architect Solon S. Beman.

Q: Where was the Washington Park race track located, and what social event became an essential aspect of a day at the races for Chicago's elite?

A: The track was located in Washington Park, between the Midway and Garfield Boulevard. All day before the races, spectators lined the streets, hoping for a glimpse of the Palmers, the Pullmans, or the Fields as they arrived at the park in carriages.

1887

The *Chicago Daily News* assigned Finley Peter Dunne to cover baseball, making him the nation's first full-time sports columnist.

Q: Dunne is credited with coining the term *southpaw* for a left-handed pitcher. How did he come up with the expression?

A: According to historian Donald Miller, it was because the orientation of Chicago's ballpark meant that a left-handed pitcher would send the ball to the plate from the south side.

1887

The world's first softball game was played on Thanksgiving in the Farragut Boat Club along the South Side lakefront.

Q: The game of softball is a distinctly Chicago invention. Softball may be its official name, but what are some of its nicknames?

A: Mushball, cabbageball, and Windy City softball.

1889

Fireworks lit up the sky when the Chicago White Stockings, led by Cap Anson, were greeted on their return from a foreign tour. Thousands of exuberant fans escorted the team to a celebration at the Palmer House.

1892

On October 1 University of Chicago coach Amos Alonzo Stagg, the nation's first tenured professor of "physical culture," began football practice on a playing area called Marshall's Field after the man who had given the land to the university.

Q: Stagg's "Ten Commandments" of a good football player included all but which of the following?

1. To help the other fellow.
2. To win.
3. To not complain, whine, or quit.
4. To pray each day.
5. To behave like a gentleman.

A: Number 2. Victory was not among his commandments. He believed the chief function of sports was to build character.

Q: Stagg's contributions to intercollegiate football included all but which of the following?

1. Putting numbers on the backs of players' jerseys so they could be identified.
2. Awarding college letters to honor outstanding players.
3. Using cheerleaders to whip up fans' enthusiasm.
4. Introducing the tackling dummy to practice.
5. Adding the huddle and the T-formation to play on the field.

A: Number 3. Stagg's emphasis was on character, not artificial enthusiasm.

Q: Stagg lived to be 102 years old and coached at several other schools after his forced retirement from the University of Chicago. The stadium built on Marshall's Field that was eventually renamed in Stagg's honor became world famous for what nonathletic event?
A: In 1941 Enrico Fermi and a group of physicists achieved the first sustained nuclear reaction in a laboratory constructed beneath the Stagg Field grandstands.

The athletic field is one of the University's laboratories and by no means the least important one.
WILLIAM RAINEY HARPER, FOUNDING PRESIDENT
OF THE UNIVERSITY OF CHICAGO

1892

Mayor Hempstead Washburne ordered Garfield Park Race Track shut down when neighbors complained of the unwholesome characters the field attracted. Owners Alderman "Bathhouse" John Coughlin and gambling boss Mike

McDonald opened the park anyway, and in a shooting melee, both a police officer and James Brown, a visiting horsebreeder from Texas, were killed.

1892

The country's first 18-hole golf course was established in Wheaton. It was called the Chicago Golf Club. By the turn of the century Chicago boasted a dozen such courses.

1892

Sunday baseball was introduced by the National League. A new baseball field for the Chicago White Stockings opened on the near West Side in order to attract and accommodate a greater number of fans.

1893

The Columbian Exposition's most uplifting entertainment was a ride on the Ferris wheel designed by an engineer named George Ferris.

Q: All but which of the following were true of the Ferris wheel?

1. Its 36 cars carried up to 60 people each.
2. For 50 cents, riders went around twice and spent 20 minutes on board.
3. As the world's tallest building at the time was only 21 stories, the Ferris wheel took riders higher than it was possible to go except in a hot air balloon.
4. The Ferris wheel stayed on the midway until it was taken down and moved to the St. Louis Fair of 1904.

A: All but number 4. After the exposition the Ferris wheel was moved to an amusement park on Clark and Diversey, then moved again to St. Louis. When that fair was over, the wheel was disassembled and sold as scrap metal.

Q: How much revenue could the Ferris wheel produce?
A: If all 36 cars were full, the Ferris wheel could hold 2,160 people; at 50 cents each that comes to $1,080 for each double turn of the wheel.

1894

The United States Golf Association was formed by the Brookline, Chicago, St. Andrews, Shinnecock, and Newport Golf Clubs.

1895

Arnold Schwinn established his bicycle company, providing vehicles for a country gone mad with "wheeling." Chicago's park and boulevard system, with its flat terrain, made cycling particularly popular. "Wheelmen" formed bicycling clubs, each with its own colors, and even women took up the fad. Bloomers and divided skirts liberated them from tightly laced Victorian clothing.

Q: What new crime did cycling add to the repertoire of the city's lawless?
A: Bicycle theft and a resulting black market became a thriving business.

1897

Albert Spalding was known as baseball's "Big Mogul" because he not only helped make baseball a respectable pastime but because he became a millionaire through the several sports-related companies he started.

Q: What were some of Spalding's companies?
A: The Spalding Company, a chief supplier of baseballs, the American Sport Publishing Company, and another company that made bicycles.

Baseball as presently conducted is a gigantic monopoly, intolerant of opposition and run on a grab-all-there-is-in-sight basis.
CAP ANSON ON HIS RETIREMENT IN 1897

1900

Charles A. Comiskey moved his baseball team to Chicago, borrowed the name of a then defunct team, and the Chicago White Sox were born. The Comiskey family would control the White Sox for more than half a century.

Q: Where did the team come from, and what was its original name?
A: Chicago native (and alderman's son) Comiskey had founded the team in St. Paul as the Saints.

Q: What was the original name of the league in which the White Sox played, and what innovative baseball event was Comiskey responsible for?
A: The White Sox originally played in the Western League. At Comiskey's urging the name was changed to the American League, and in 1903 the National League granted the upstarts full status by agreeing to a playoff to be known as the World Series—all at Comiskey's behest.

1901

The White Sox won the American League Pennant.

1902

The Cubs name was first applied to the baseball team that then played on the West Side, and the Cubs famous combo of shortstop Joe Tinker, second baseman Johnny Evers, and first baseman Frank Chance first played together.

Q: What were some of the other names the Cubs had been known by?
A: The Colts and the Orphans.

Q: How did the Cubs get their name?
A: Legend has it that the name was first assigned the team in an unnamed sports column in the *Chicago Daily News.*

Q: What did Tinker, Evers, and Chance do so well that they became immortalized in a poem?
A: They made double plays so smoothly that sportswriter Franklin P. Adams wrote a poem about them in 1906.

Trio of bear Cubs, and fleeter than birds,
Tinker to Evers to Chance.
Thoughtlessly pricking our gonfalon bubble,
Making a great hit into a double,
Words that are weighty with nothing but trouble,
Tinker to Evers to Chance.

FRANKLIN P. ADAMS

1904

Riverview Park opened. For over 60 years it remained one of Chicago's favorite attractions and one of the country's most famous amusement parks.

Q: Where was Riverview located, and what is there now?
A: Riverview extended from Western Avenue to the Chicago River along Belmont. It's now the site of DeVry Institute of Technology and a shopping center.

Q: What were Riverview's origins?
A: It began before the turn of the century as a club for skeet shooters. The owners converted it to a full-scale amusement park in 1904.

Q: Riverview wasn't always Chicago's most popular amusement park. What park had held that title earlier?
A: The White City, located at 63rd and Cottage Grove, opened in 1905, a year after Riverview. Numerous fires and the depression led to its closing in 1933 and demolition a few years later.

1906

The first "subway" World Series occurred in Chicago between the White Sox and Cubs. It was also the last series between these two teams.

Q: Which team won?
A: The Cubs were favored, but the White Sox won in six games.

1908

The National Amateur Playground Ball Association of the United States was established in Chicago to encourage and regulate the game of softball.

1909

The first automobile license was issued in Chicago.

Q: America's first automobile race had been held in Chicago. When was it held, and who raced in it?
A: The event started at the Palace of Fine Arts—now the Museum of Science and Industry—and ran up to Evanston. In 1945 winner J. Frank Duryea came to Chicago to rerun the race as part of a museum event.

1910

On July 1 the Chicago White Sox played their first game in Comiskey Park, one of only three steel and concrete stadiums in the country. The others were all made of wood.

Q: What team did they play, and who won?
A: They lost to the St. Louis Browns, 2-0.

1911

Jack Johnson, who spent his last years in Chicago and is buried in Graceland Cemetery, moved to Chicago. The next year, he became the first black heavyweight champion of the world.

Q: Johnson lost the title a few years later under suspicious circumstances. What were they?
A: Rumors of bribery surrounded his defeat by Jess Willard in 1915.

Q: What business did Johnson start in Chicago?
A: He opened an interracial nightclub just south of the Levee district called Cafe Champion.

1914

Weeghman Park opened at Clark and Addison as home to a short-lived baseball team. Five years later, a group of Chicagoans purchased a West Side team originally known as the White Stockings from the Taft family of Cincinnati and moved it into Weeghman Park.

Q: Where was the team's original home?
A: It was a field on the West Side at Polk and Wolcott Streets.

Q: What team was the field built for, and who was it named after?
A: Built in 1914 for a Federal League team called the Whales, it was originally named for the team's owner, Charles Weeghman, a Chicago restaurateur. The team folded after two seasons.

Q: Who was in the group that bought the Cubs in 1919?
A: It included J. Ogden Armour (of the meatpacking family), who persuaded William Wrigley Jr. (founder of the chewing gum business) to invest in it. Though Wrigley wasn't a baseball fan, he felt the team should be locally owned. Eventually he acquired a majority interest.

Q: When did the field get its present name?
A: Weeghman Park became Wrigley Field in 1926. The Wrigley family owned the team for over 60 years.

1919

In professional sports' most infamous incident, eight members of the Chicago White Sox agreed to lose the World Series game in return for a cash payment.

Q: What was this incident called, and what were the reasons behind it?
A: The Black Sox Scandal involved, in addition to "Shoeless" Joe Jackson, eight players including Happy Felsch, Ed Sciotte, Lefty Williams, and Buck Weaver among others. The players succumbed to bribery because they felt the salaries Comiskey paid were inadequate.

Q: Who was it who bribed the "Black Sox"?
A: A consortium of East Coast gamblers led by Arnold Rothstein.

Q: What was "Shoeless" Joe Jackson noted for in addition to his incomparable talent as a hitter?
A: He never learned to read or write. Some historians believe the inferiority engendered by his illiteracy may have been one of his reasons for throwing the series.

Q: The man who became baseball commissioner at the height of the scandal had a distinctive name. Who was he, and how did he get his name?

A: Kenesaw Mountain Landis—his first name came from a Civil War battle—had been a federal judge in Chicago before he became baseball commissioner. His most famous legal decision involved the sentencing of labor leader "Big Bill" Haywood to 20 years in prison for pacifism.

1920

A former University of Illinois football star named George Halas hooked up with a Decatur starch maker named A. E. Staley and got him to support a football team during baseball's off season. The connection provided a start for a man who became known as "the winningest coach in football."

Q: How had Halas begun his career in professional sports?
A: As a right fielder for the New York Yankees.

Q: The Chicago Bears might never have existed had Halas not missed a famous boat. What was the boat?
A: On July 24, 1915, young Halas, like many of his Czech neighbors who worked for the Western Electric company, was set to go on a lake outing aboard the Eastland. Luckily for Halas, he arrived too late to board—the ship capsized at its berth in the Chicago River, killing 800 people.

Q: How did the Chicago Bears get their name?
A: In a playful nod to the Chicago Cubs, Halas renamed his team the Chicago Bears.

Q: Under George Halas the Bears became the first team to film and study its games, hire its own band, and publish a team newspaper.
He also introduced which of the following?

1. He pushed for rule changes that allowed for more forward passing.
2. He introduced the T-formation.
3. He recommended that throwing the football from behind the line of scrimmage be legalized.
4. He insisted that no player could be signed until he completed college.

A: All of the above.

Q: Where did the Bears play before the team moved to Soldier Field?
A: For exactly 50 years, beginning in 1921, the Bears played at Wrigley Field.

Q: Halas not only founded the Bears, but played as well. What record did he make that stood until 1972?

A: He recovered a fumble and outran Jim Thorpe for 93 yards.

Q: What was the original name of the Chicago Bears?

A: The Decatur Staleys.

1925

University of Illinois star running back Red "the Galloping Ghost" Grange so captured the national imagination on the playing field that George Halas offered him the then unheard figure of $25,000 per year to play for the Bears. In one stroke professional football became a legitimate big-time professional sport.

If you have the football and eleven guys are after you, if you're smart, you'll run.

HAROLD "RED" GRANGE

Football isn't meant to be played for money.

BOB ZUPPKE, COACH OF BOTH GEORGE HALAS AND
RED GRANGE AT THE UNIVERSITY OF ILLINOIS

1926

A Chicago basketball coach named Abe Saperstein put together a team whose basketball-handling skills and humor were so striking, he diverted them from serious play into the world of entertainment. He called them the Harlem Globetrotters.

Q: What famous baseball star once played for the Harlem Globetrotters?

A: Ernie Banks, who later became known as "Mr. Cub."

1927

Gene Tunney defeated Jack Dempsey in Soldier Field on September 22 in one of boxing's most controversial bouts. After a knockdown the referee gave Tunney a "long count" that enabled him to come back and turn the tide of the match.

1929

The Cubs won the National League Pennant.

1930

Chicago Cub Hack Wilson set the National League record for home runs at 56.

1930

Chicago native Johnny Weissmuller converted his swimming triumphs at the 1924 and 1928 Olympic games to cash when he was signed to play Tarzan in the movies.

> *I went to the back lot at MGM. They gave me a G-string and said, "Can you climb a tree? Can you pick up that girl?" I could do all that.*
> JOHNNY WEISSMULLER, CONCERNING HIS SCREEN TEST FOR *TARZAN*

Q: Weissmuller later trained for the role in a famous moorish-style pool in Chicago? Where was it?
A: In the Medinah Athletic Club, now the Hotel Inter-Continental, on Michigan Avenue.

1932

The Cubs again won the National League Pennant.

1933

The first aerial tramway in the world offered rides at the Century of Progress fair in Chicago.

1933

The Amateur Softball Association was founded in Chicago. Now headquartered in Oklahoma, it grew to become the largest membership organization recognized by the U.S. Olympic Committee.

1935

For the third time in six years, the Cubs topped the National League.

1935

Jay Berwanger won the first ever Heisman Trophy for his play at the University of Chicago.

> *There is no doubt that, on the whole, football has been a major handicap to education in the United States.*
> ROBERT MAYNARD HUTCHINS, PRESIDENT OF THE UNIVERSITY OF CHICAGO,
> ON ABOLISHING THE UNIVERSITY'S FOOTBALL PROGRAM IN 1939

1936

Chicagoans Jesse Owens and Ralph Metcalfe brought home gold medals from the Olympic games in Berlin.

Q: What made the their accomplishments particularly striking?

A: Adolf Hitler had staged the Olympics in Berlin to showcase Aryan superiority. When black Americans dominated the track events, Hitler stalked out.

First you must dream. It all begins with the dream.

JESSE OWENS

1938

The Chicago Blackhawks won the Stanley Cup.

1940

Jack Brickhouse broadcasted Cubs and White Sox games for 41 years (1940-81) with only brief breaks at other stations and to serve in the marines in World War II. He is said to have seen 5,300 games.

Q: What was Brickhouse's broadcast trademark?

A: "Hey-hey," first uttered during the 1950s when Hank Sauer hit a home run.

Q: Though built like a house of bricks, that's not how he got his name. What was?

A: His vaudevillian father's relationship with his mother—a coal miner's daughter—lasted only long enough for her to acquire his name, which originally was Steinhausen and which was translated into Brickhouse.

1945

Sam "Billy Goat" Sianis put a curse on the Cubs after he and his goat were ejected from Wrigley Field during the World Series. So far the curse has worked—the Cubs have not since returned to the World Series.

Q: What business was Sianis in?

A: A restaurateur, he established a subterranean restaurant below Michigan Avenue that soon became famous as a hangout for journalists.

Q: For what expression is Sianis's restaurant famous today?

A: "Cheese-booga, cheese-booga, Pepsi no Coke," made immortal on *Saturday Night Live* by Chicagoan John Belushi.

1947

Playing in Comiskey Park, the Chicago Cardinals won their first—and only—NFL championship.

1951

Sam Snead became the only person ever to hit the Wrigley Field scoreboard when—as a promotional stunt—he used a 2-iron on a golf ball prior to the season opener.

1959

Bill Veeck Jr. bought the Chicago White Sox and the team won the American League pennant for the first time in 40 years.

Q: The White Sox was the not the first team Veeck had run. Name the others?

A: The Milwaukee Brewers, the Cleveland Indians, and the St. Louis Browns.

Q: Veeck's ownership of the White Sox was not the first Veeck family involvement with Chicago baseball. Name the other.

A: Veeck's father, William Sr., was president of the Chicago Cubs in the 1920s, enabling Bill Jr. to become one of the first Cub bat boys.

Q: What other famous Chicagoan also served as a Cub bat boy?

A: Newscaster/journalist Walter Jacobson.

1961

The Blackhawks again won the Stanley Cup.

1963

Not only did the Bears lead the NFL, but Loyola's team won basketball's N.I.T. title.

1965

Leo Dorocher managed the Cubs to their first finish in the first-division in 20 years.

Show me a good loser ... and I'll show you an idiot!

LEO DOROCHER

1966

A new basketball team began playing in Chicago—the Bulls.

1967

Riverview, still remembered as the world's largest amusement park, announced it would not open the following year. Closed-door deal-making involving Daley cronies and park district commissioner Jacob Arvey were rumored to be behind a plan to turn the huge park into an industrial mall. It was the end not only of a popular attraction but of the era of the urban amusement park.

Q: Riverview's glory days lasted from the 1930s until the 1950s. What were some of the rides?
A: The Bobs, a thrilling roller-coaster ride that was considered America's fastest until 1959, a spook house called Aladdin's Castle, the Silver Streak roller-coaster—one of nine—and the Pair-o-Chutes, a thrilling 212-foot drop in a gondola suspended under a parachute.

Q: Riverview also had a culinary distinction. What was it?
A: In the 1930s it acquired another superlative by selling the nation's first 12-inch "foot-long" hot dogs.

1975

The Chicago Bulls scored their highest point total in a single game—152—only to lose every single game they played in November of the next year.

Q: During the 1970s, the Bulls had their first superstar. Who was he, and where is he now?
A: Bob Love is now the community relations spokesperson for the Bulls.

1977

Chicago Bear Walter Payton set the NFL record for most yards in a single game when he gained 275 yards against the Minnesota Vikings on November 20.

Q: Payton also holds the NFL record for the most career touchdowns rushing. How many did he score?
A: Payton zipped into the end zone 110 times between 1975 and 1987.

1980

The longest game in Cub history was played on July 6. It lasted 5 hours, 31 minutes and 20 innings before the Cubs finally lost to the Pittsburgh Pirates 5-4.

1982

On September 5, Northwestern University ended the worst losing streak in big-school college football history—40 consecutive defeats.

Q: What team did they defeat to end the drought?
A: Northern Illinois University.

1982

A young team called the Sting took the North American Soccer League championship.

1984

The Chicago Cubs set the all-time attendance record at Wrigley Field.

Q: What was the attraction for the Cubs that year?
A: They won their first National League title in four decades, but lost the National League playoffs to the San Diego Padres.

1986

The Bears defeated the New England Patriots 46-10 in Super Bowl XX. It was the team's only Super Bowl appearance.

Go out and play Bear football, smart and aggressive. If something bad happens, don't worry. Why? Because we're in this together. We are going to win it for each other.

MIKE DITKA, URGING THE BEARS TO WIN
THEIR FIRST SUPER BOWL VICTORY

Q: How many NFL championships have the Chicago Bears won?
A: Depending on one's interpretation, either seven or nine: in 1921, 1932, 1933, 1940, 1941, 1943, 1946, 1963, and 1986. Their first two championships were won before the team was called the Bears and before the league title became official.

Q: When was the last championship under founding coach George Halas?
A: In 1963 with a team that included Johnny Morris and Mike Ditka, the team won a comeback title for 68-year-old "Pappa Bear" Halas.

1989

After a long and hard battle with neighborhood residents, the Cubs became the last major league team to introduce night baseball on their home field.

1991

After much hand-wringing by Chicago media, the Chicago Bears often-maligned owner Mike McCaskey fired coach Mike Ditka. Jerry Reinsdorf, the occasionally maligned owner of the Sox and the Bulls, celebrated the opening of the new Comiskey Park, which has also drawn a fair amount of criticism.

1994

Soldier Field hosted the first World Cup Soccer match to be played on American soil.

Q: The Chicago Park District owns Soldier Field. What other sporting venues are part of its 7,300-acre system?
A: In all, 29 miles of lakefront, 563 parks, 817 baseball diamonds, and 706 tennis courts.

1996

The Chicago Bulls, led by celestials Michael Jordon, Scottie Pippen, and Dennis Rodman, won their fourth NBA title in six years.

BIBLIOGRAPHY AND
BOOKS FOR BROWSING

Our list of sources for this book are many and varied; since both of us grew up in Chicago, we've been gathering this information for longer than we can recall. We also have both written and/or edited several other books about the city, and information and insights gathered for those naturally made their way into this book as well. Specifically, in gathering facts for this book we consulted the volumes listed below. Sometimes our sources didn't agree, so we went with what seemed right. Any errors are, of course, our responsibility.

As we got into this process, we realized that though some aspects of Chicago's past—architecture, commerce, journalism and literature, the 1920s, 20th-century politics, professional sports—are well documented, others are not. There's very little information available, for example, on either 19th-century politics or the performing arts in Chicago. Though our self-image likely explains the latter omission, it doesn't explain the former.

We hope this little volume will enticed readers to learn more about Chicago's extraordinary history—and browsing through the following books is a great way to begin.

—Connie Goddard and Bruce Boyer

Andrews, Clarence. *Literary Chicago.* Iowa City: Midwest Heritage Publishing Company, 1982.

Badger, R. Reid. *The Great American Fair: The World's Columbian Exposition and American Culture.* Chicago: Nelson-Hall, 1979.

Bonner, Thomas Neville. *Medicine in Chicago, 1850-1950.* Madison: American History Research Center, 1957.

A Business Tour of Chicago, Depicting Fifty Years' Progress. Chicago: E. E. Barton, 1887.

City of Chicago, Department of Development and Planning. *Historic City: The Settlement of Chicago.* Chicago: City of Chicago, 1976a.

_____. *The People of Chicago—Who We Are and Who We Have Been: Census Data on Foreign Born, Foreign Stock and Race, 1837-1970.* Chicago: City of Chicago, 1976b.

Cronon, William. *Nature's Metropolis: Chicago and the Great West.* New York: W. W. Norton, 1991.

Darby, Edwin. *The Fortune Builders.* Garden City, N.Y.: Doubleday & Company, 1986.

DeBartolo, Joseph A. *The Original Chicago Trivia Book.* Chicago: Sarsaparilla, Ltd., 1985.

Ebner, Michael. *Chicago's North Shore.* Chicago: University of Chicago Press, 1988.

Edgerton, Michael and Heise, Kenan. *Chicago: Center for Enterprise.* Woodland Hills, CA: Windsor Publications, 1982.

Hayner, Don, and Tom McNamee. *Streetwise Chicago: A History of Chicago Street Names.* Chicago: Loyola University Press, 1988.

_____. *Metro Chicago Almanac.* Chicago: Bonus Books and Chicago Sun-Times, 1991.

Heise, Kenan. *The Chicagoization of America, 1893-1917.* Evanston, IL: Chicago Historical Bookworks, 1990.

_____. and Ed Baumann. *Chicago Originals.* Chicago: Bonus Books, 1990.

_____. and Mark Frazel. *Hands on Chicago.* Chicago: Bonus Books, 1987.

Johnson, Curt, with Sautter, R. Craig. *Wicked City.* Highland Park, IL: December Press, 1994.

Lindberg, Richard C. *Chicago by Gaslight.* Chicago: Academy Chicago Books, 1996.

_____. *Ethnic Chicago: A Complete Guide to the Many Faces & Cultures of Chicago.* Lincolnwood, IL: Passport Books, 1993.

_____. *Quotable Chicago.* Chicago: Loyola Press, Wild Onion Books, 1996.

Long, Dolores A. *The Chicago Trivia Book.* Chicago: Contemporary Books, Inc., 1982.

Mark, Norman. *Mayors, Madams, and Madmen.* Chicago: Chicago Review Press, 1979.

Mayer, Harold M., and Richard C. Wade. *Chicago: Growth of a Metropolis.* Chicago: University of Chicago Press, 1986.

McCarthy, Kathleen D. *Noblesse Oblige: Charity & Cultural Philanthropy in Chicago, 1849-1929.* Chicago: University of Chicago Press, 1982.

Miller, Donald L. *City of the Century: The Epic of Chicago and the Making of America.* New York: Simon & Schuster, 1996.

Municipal Reference Library, Frederick Rex, Librarian. *Centennial List of Mayors, Aldermen and Other Elective Officials, 1837-1937.* City of Chicago, 1937.

Pacyga, Dominic A., and Ellen Skerrett. *Chicago: City of Neighborhoods.* Chicago: Loyola University Press, 1986.

Regnery, Henry. *Creative Chicago.* Chicago: Chicago Historical Bookworks, 1993.

Rowe, Mike. *Chicago Blues: The City & the Music.* New York: A La Capo Press, 1975.

Sawyers, June Skinner. *Chicago Portraits: Biographies of 250 Famous Chicagoans.* Chicago: Loyola University Press, 1991.

_____. *Chicago Sketches: Urban Tales, Stories and Legends from Chicago History.* Chicago: Loyola Press, Wild Onion Books, 1995.

Sinkevitch, Alice, and AIA. *The AIA Guide to Chicago.* San Diego: Harcourt Brace with the American Institute of Architects, 1993.

Sturdy, Alan, ed. *The Chicago Story.* Chicago: Chicago Association of Commerce and Industry, 1954.

Survey of Chicago. Chicago: Chicago Association of Commerce & Industry, 1925.

Wagenknecht, Edward. *Chicago.* Norman, OK: University of Oklahoma Press, 1964.

Washburn, Charles. *Come into My Parlor: A Biography of the Aristocratic Everleigh Sisters.* New York: National Library Press, 1936.

Willie, Lois. *Forever Open, Clear and Free: The Struggle for Chicago's Lakefront,* 2nd ed. Chicago: University of Chicago Press, 1991.